RESULTS-DRIVEN
EVENT
PLANNING

Using Marketing Tools to

Boost Your Bottom Line

INGRID E. LUNDQUIST, CSEP

TLC PUBLISHING   ROSEVILLE, CA

RESULTS-DRIVEN EVENT PLANNING: Using Marketing Tools to Boost Your Bottom Line
Copyright ©2011 by Ingrid E. Lundquist, CSEP

Printed in the United State of America. First printing 2011

Cover design: Vanessa Perez

Cover photo: MK Shannon

ISBN 978-1-936616-00-8

Events 2. Business 3.marketing   1. Title

For permission requests, write the publisher, "Attention: Permissions Coordinator," at the address below or the email address. Requests for quantity discounts and speaking engagements should be made via email to i.lundquist@events-TLC.com

TLC Publishing
P.O. Box 542
Roseville, CA 95661
(916) 797-5337
www.TLCpublishing.com

For more information on events, visit The Lundquist Company at www.events-TLC.com.

Check out the other publications from TLC Publishing at www.TLCPublishing.com

DEDICATION

To my mom and mentor, Jessamine Lee Lundquist, the person who got me started in events, and who was the volunteer wedding coordinator at the First Presbyterian Church in San Mateo for 35 years; and to her best friend, fellow planner, and my dear friend Doris Bohn, who recently handed down her party punch bowl to me, and to her husband Eddie who gladly carried it to my car.

And to my dad, George Carl Lundquist, with whom I agree that the experience of being there is the best education.

CONTENTS

- Room and table setup
- Expect the unexpected
- Name badges
- Wine glasses, napkins, and food
- Leftover food and product – count backwards
- Unused dinner napkins
- Overflowing garbage
- Culling the photographs

- Rededication of Matthew Kilgore Cemetery
- City of Rancho Cordova 5th Anniversary
- The Firehouse Restaurant 50th Anniversary
- First 5 Sacramento Children's Celebration

- Do you have the stamina?
- Where are the jobs?
- Tips on how to ensure success
- The next great idea is in your bathtub

FOREWORD

Event professionals often ask me what they can do to create events that are strategic, successful and fun. They want to be the event professionals who are brought back repeatedly to handle events because they have solid reputations for creativity, reliability and fiscal responsibility. And they want to win the *Special Events Magazine* Gala Award, which recognizes superior event work from throughout the world.

I have a simple answer for this question: Create events the way Ingrid Lundquist does.

I have known Ingrid for more than a decade, and have always been impressed by the clear thinking and broad perspective she brings to her events. Her events have goals that are achieved, and the guests have fun all along the way.

With this book, Ingrid shares her comprehensive approach to designing and producing events. Not only will it give you new ways of looking at event design and production, it will also help you avoid mistakes that could jeopardize both your event and your reputation.

Consider it an MBA course in event production. I know you will graduate with honors.

Lisa Hurley

Editor

Special Events Magazine

PREFACE

"You always amaze."
   — Stephen Revetria,
      Vice President & General Manager
      Giants Enterprises

People who design great events are often creative thinkers who shy away from corporate events, because their expertise is not in business. Ask them to create a marketing plan, business plan or any kind of plan, and their eyes quickly search for the closest exit. With two art degrees and an English degree under my belt, I naturally gravitated toward corporate event production and marketing. Naturally, you say, doesn't make sense. I already had a love of throwing parties, running parades and coordinating fashion shows, but I noted that some were more successful than others. I dipped my toes into the public relations industry to learn about the media and writing press releases.

Marketing was one of those words that no one I knew had any idea what it meant. Even people that were hanging shingles positioning them as marketing experts couldn't really explain what it was. Then one day about 15 years ago, I was on the board of a professional organization, and we were having a meeting in a conference room at Hewlett Packard. The topic was that the organization needed a marketing plan to attract and retain members. Most people around the table had never created a marketing plan.

As the group leader explained the words goal, objective, strategy and tactics in layman's terms, creating a marketing plan became a doable idea. The plan came together and was successful. I felt the results were primarily due to an understanding of how the pieces fit together in a particular order, and that consequences were predetermined. We knew where we were going, and we knew what we wanted to accomplish. Now that the mystery of the "Marketing Plan" had been revealed, it was not frightening at all, but rather a straightforward way to accomplish a task.

There was simplicity in the way I now understood the workings of marketing, and I wondered if that simplicity could be applied to producing events with the same success rate. I immediately began applying marketing techniques to event production, and created "results-driven events." When the plan is followed, you can count on results.

Since 2001, I've been teaching these techniques to the extension students at the University of California, Davis in their Marketing Certificate program. Many of these students are sent to the class by their employers because their company is having an event, and someone needs to be in charge. The students enter the class either with fear in their eyes or with a cocky belief that they know everything there is to know about events. In the end, the fear is replaced with confidence, and the cockiness with a deep respect for the intricate world of events.

The words on these pages are written in a manner that you should find easy to understand, and I've used examples that are more general than obscure. This volume doesn't proclaim to be a book written for the intellectual or the seasoned professional event producer. It is a book written for people who want practical information written in an easy-to-read style and format. The information was compiled from lectures, handouts and presentations, given both in the UC Davis class and at professional conventions and guest speaking engagements over the years. Although the information has a corporate undertone, the concepts can be applied to social, non-profit or family events, large and small; any gathering with people, food, and entertainment or activity.

Results-Driven Event Planning is your guide to producing successful events time-after-time.

Enjoy.

THE PROCESS OF PLANNING
AND BUILDING
RESULTS-DRIVEN EVENTS

In the event industry, it is common knowledge that the presentation of the 1984 Olympic Games held in Los Angeles was a pivotal milestone in the world of events. The defining word was *sponsorship*. Positioning a product with the activity of its audience would cause rise to a brand-new industry that directly linked the product to the end user, using an event as the common ground.

The concept was simple. Let's say I sell running shoes; if I sponsor a marathon the attendees will see my logo and connect with my brand. If I have a tent where the attendees gather and can try on the shoes, better still. I don't have to advertise to the general population because most of those people won't buy my product — I just need to market to the people who are likely to purchase my product. I have to figure out where my buyers will be and be there too. We know this as *target marketing:* using event sponsorships as the vehicle to get you so close to your audience you can actually touch them.

In a short period of time, connecting product marketing to events through sponsorships positioned events as a viable marketing tool. Events continue to be a mainstay of today's marketing mix, and planners who capitalize on applying this time-tested marketing methodology to their event design can count on success.

Like any good recipe, it may take some tweaking to fine-tune the ingredients, but the basic elements of a marketing plan provide the base structure required to begin developing your event plan. Since the expected outcome of a marketing plan is results, it makes sense to refer to the application of the marketing plan to the event design as a *results-driven event plan.*

Creating a marketing plan for a party, get-together, or mixer simply sounds lightweight. Let the folks planning those events bake and frost cupcakes; we have business to attend to. We need a plan for our results-driven event.

You don't need a degree in marketing to understand how to apply a marketing plan to an event. You do need a solid event plan. To boost your bottom line results, you have to follow through with the plan.

To that end, we start with the basic elements of a marketing plan, then weave them into an event plan. Every entry on your event plan will find its proper place within the structure of an event.

From the event perspective, you're familiar with the words *invitation, music, food,* and *parking,* and from the marketing side you've heard the words *goal, objective, strategy,* and *tactic.* In the following pages you'll find more words and terms specific to the marketing and event industries, which will be helpful as you build your plan for a results-driven event.

I coined the term *results-driven events* because it means what it says and is more likely to receive corporate recognition than an agenda item about party-planning. However, you'll find that while this information is directed toward business events, the concept and process applies effectively to church socials, family reunions, non-profit fundraisers, and just about any gathering of people.

When you think about the elements of any event, they are similar whether the event is corporate or social.

The primary elements of an event include:
- Communicating with the guests in the form of an invitation or announcement
- Food and beverage
- Restrooms
- Entertainment and activities
- Safety and security
- Permits and insurance
- Venue and parking

SIMPLIFIED MARKETING LINGO

If you're new to marketing or have suddenly been placed in the position of working with a marketing team, one way to strengthen your position is to understand what your colleagues are saying by learning their lingo. Below are some basic phrases and terms used in marketing, but keep in mind that every corporate environment will have its own personalized jargon, which you'll hear repeated in formal meetings and informal hallway conversations.

Create a list of words specific to your company or client and make sure you know both the meaning of the words as they are used by the speaker and the nuances of the words in the context of the discussion.

(Listed in the order that you might hear the terms as they relate to events)

Keywords: *corporate, families, friendly, stylish, opulent*

Be conscious of words your client tends to repeat in reference to his company and event. These are the words you'll want to keep at the forefront when developing the design of the event.

Brand: *reflects who you are — from your internal motivation to your external presentation.*

Understand your client's brand inside and out because a *strong brand mirrors its audience.*

It's not a party, get that word out of your head. It's a business event with a beginning, a middle, and an end. And, whoever hired you or assigned you this project expects you to produce results, hence, results-driven events.

Integrated Marketing Team: *Members may include representatives from internal departments (within your client's company, such as Human Resources, IT, Sales, Facilities, or Operations) or external sources (services contracted by the company, such as advertising and public relations firms).* The same department, or contractor, does not always take the lead in every project, but as individual departments and contractors, they retain their same ultimate goal while adding their capabilities to the overall project.

Example:

The Human Resources Department is interested in the employees. The facilities manager is interested in maintaining the working order of the building. The public relations firm is interested in gaining publicity for the client and promoting the product. It is imperative to understand the underlying goal of each member of the team in the beginning, so that as you develop your event, you can include his or her primary desire in the plan.

Bandwidth: the capability to produce the desired product (knowledge, staff, resources, etc.).

Example:
Your project needs 50 people to greet guests, but the marketing department can only supply 40 people as greeters; therefore, the department does not have the bandwidth to provide the service.

Solution:
Recognizing this shortcoming at an early stage of the planning process allows the planner to augment the needed staffing from another source to meet the required number of greeters.

Crowd and event accommodations covers the basic human safety and maintenance requirements of food, water, shelter, restrooms, security, etc

Crowd/Event Accommodations: another phrase coined by the author to reflect the necessities required to fulfill the needs of the audience (the crowd) and the production (the event) elements.

Example:
The event has a band requiring a performance area (stage) and the audience needs a place to view the performance (seating).
➤ Crowd (seating)/event (stage)

The age old question — do you want it or do you need it?

Needs Assessment: goods and services needed to produce the event. You know you need things to produce the event. The needs assessment builds a list of what you specifically will require for each element of the event.

Example:

Your audience requires seating. Although you may want overstuffed leather lounge chairs, you need seating for 500, which could be in the form of folding chairs, benches, bleachers, or a designated lawn area.

The needs assessment is a valuable phrase to reference when someone tries to lead the event discussion in a direction that will negatively impact the budget. Conversely, budgeting on the low end for a necessary item leaves room for an upgrade if you come in under budget on another item.

Example:

You are expecting a crowd of 500 people at a public event in a downtown area at lunchtime, and you anticipate they will need to eat. Your planning team may want to serve hot meals to the guests, but only funds for snacks are in the budget. Since independent concession trucks are already permitted downtown, alerting them about your event will allow the attendees to purchase hot food, if they choose, or consume your cold snacks.

SWOT Analysis: Strengths, Weaknesses, Opportunities, and Threats

Strengths and weaknesses are internal considerations. They are the good and bad that come with the project.

Strengths and weaknesses can be tangibles, like an in-house graphics department with commercial presses, or intangible, such as the relationship of a board member whose best friend owns a sports team.

Although the in-house graphics department sounds convenient and is free, the work they put out may look stale and dated. The only problem with the sports team is that your senior-aged audience may not respond to a soccer superstar as a guest speaker because soccer wasn't a part of their life growing up. See how it works?

Be wary of gifts you don't need.

Strengths (internal): large event budget, free, fenced, corporate grounds where the event will be held

Weaknesses (internal): limited setup staff, no kitchen

Opportunities and threats are external considerations over which you have little or no control. What you do have control over is your ability to make an effort to foresee potential challenges and have a plan in place to meet the challenges.

Opportunities (external): good weather for an outdoor event, easy access for delivery trucks

Threats (external): breaking news, bad neighborhood, huge event scheduled for the same day (thus no rental tents or chairs available)

Think of the gap in your event design as an opportunity to uncover an exciting and memorable addition to your original event plan

Gap Analysis: identifies the "gap" or holes in your plan.

Example:

Your company is planning a large event on a vacant lot at the back of the property where your main warehouse is located. The event site is free; restrooms, running water, and electricity are located in your warehouse; and, most importantly, your boss wants to bring customers to his facility. The problem is that the parking lot is full during normal business hours.

Solution — options:

- Hire a valet service to park the cars nearby
- Rent adjoining vacant property and hire staff to direct self-parking
- Rent off-site parking and a shuttle bus to get guests to and from the site
- Hold the event before or after business hours

The reason for the gap analysis is to identify areas of your plan that don't fit together, like pieces of a puzzle, and explore solutions to eliminate the gap.

Always search out more than one solution for the problem because a good solution has the potential of enhancing the event and making it even more memorable...perhaps the valet service or parking staff is dressed in your company's uniforms (remember branding?), perhaps the shuttle bus driver warms up the crowd with a little scripted material on the company (that's called product education), or perhaps you hold the event before or after hours and extend the invitation to the families of your customers.

Considering Opposites and Opportunity

Like strengths and weaknesses, life is filled with opposites, which impact what we do and how we think:

Talking and keeping quiet

Black and white

Outside and inside

Up and down

Going slow and rushing

Depending on the circumstance, what is considered a strength from one perspective is viewed as a weakness from another. Taking time to explore options, then making a decision based on research can sometimes result in uncovering unexpected opportunities that appear quickly and are gone just as fast. Practice will help you seize the moment and recognize surprise windfalls.

BASIC ELEMENTS OF A MARKETING PLAN

The executive summary is mentioned first in this section discussing the marketing plan because it is the culmination of the project. Everything you do leads to that document and showing results. Thinking about the executive summary in the beginning of your project provides a foundation on which to build out your ideas.

The company mission and vision statements are mentioned next because, too often in the heat of planning, you can easily forget why you are working on the project. It is important to review the mission and vision of the company before the planning process begins to ensure that your plans reflect the company, its product, and its audience.

Other topics covered in this section are culture, value and integrity. You've heard of *corporate culture*, meaning the overall atmosphere of the business. It is the essence of the corporation, and is reflected in employees' attire, their work ethic, and often their outside interests, such as philanthropy or community service. The corporate culture may have its own unique language, buzz words, or phrases easily understood among employees, whether in neighboring offices or on the other side of the world.

Spending time to understand the corporate culture of your client allows you, from the outset, to integrate it into the event design and will reduce the number of changes later in the process.

Executive Summary: a summary of findings or, in the case of the event, a summary of the event.

An executive summary often takes on the format of the person who made the assignment and who will be reading it. It contains information of interest to the reader/s. (A boss, a board, a committee, etc.)

Sometimes the executive summary is limited to one page, and sometimes it goes on for several pages. It may include bulleted lists or short paragraphs with subtitles. It also may be a string of paragraphs resembling a one-page letter.

Whatever the final format, the executive summary presents the results of the event in an abbreviated form. The information is gleaned from factual resources, such as spreadsheets, attendance lists, vendor lists, sales figures, or sponsor information.

If the final documentation includes many pages of reports, charts, lists, budgets, etc., the executive summary is often the first of the series of written documents. Photographs usually either precede or follow the text documents.

The executive summary of a project shows the bottom line results, and the bottom line came from somewhere. No matter how long or short the executive summary, acquiring and maintaining accurate supporting results documentation is critical to the integrity of your project

Mission Statement: some get wordy, but most use the fewest words possible to hone right in on exactly why you do what you do.

Starbucks' Mission Statement:[1]
Our mission: to inspire and nurture the human spirit—one person, one cup and one neighborhod at a time.

Pride Industries' Mission Statement:[2]
Our mission: Pride is people helping people realize their potential to live and work in the community

Vision Statement: what you wish to become; looking to the future and how your company fits into the world.

Starbucks' Vision Statement:[3]
To establish Starbucks as the most recognized and respected brand in the world.

Pride Industries' Vision Statement:[4]
Pride will be a visionary leader in pioneering innovative strategies and approaches to maximize personal growth and potential of the people it serves.

Values/Culture/Integrity: fundamental beliefs and ethics.

In layman's terms, these are your core beliefs — what is at the heart of your company.

---

1 www.starbucks.com
2 www.prideindustries.com
3 www.starbucks.com
4 www.prideindustries.com

Needs Assessment: *what you need to attain the objectives*

Event Analysis: *SWOT and Gap*

Research Evaluation: *summary of information gleaned from research.*

This could be listings of other events taking place on the day of your event, vendor proposal comparisons, available guest lists, etc.

A successful event mirrors its audience.

BUILDING THE EVENT PLAN

Building the event plan will follow the same guidelines as building a marketing plan. You'll need to identify the goals, objectives, strategy, and tactics. You've heard these words before in everyday language, but they are often misused, used interchangeably, or the specific meaning of each word is misunderstood.

GOAL

The dictionary definition of "goal" often references something linear or final, like crossing the finish line at the end of a race or scoring the last point in a game. In a marketing plan, and in your event plan, the goal is the big picture. It is most likely comprised of many smaller pictures.

For the creative mind assigned to plan an event, thinking of your event goal as a panorama with snapshots is less restricting and more encouraging than the perspective of a salesman who has to make that one last sale to reach his quota.

Creativity is often motivated by a structure or a foundation. The canvas is the foundation on which the artist paints, the camera captures images for a photographer, software and drafting tools aid the architect, and a good knife is the tool of the chef.

A creative mind fears restriction when thinking about the prospect of business. The creative mind thinks in unrestricted shapes. Today, his thoughts might take the shape of an oval or circle, and tomorrow, a sunburst.

The creative mind's idea may follow the undulating route of a 100-mile endurance bicycle race, or take a roller coaster loop-d-loop. It encourages discovery and allows the idea to follow its own path.

Encouraging the creative mind to think from a business perspective is far easier than teaching a business mind to be creative.

Creative people imagine that the business mind thinks in terms of boxes, right angles, and confined spaces. A corporate organization chart is usually made up of boxes with names and titles that connect to each other and indicate rank. A pie chart is circular, but still has defined angular shapes, and a bar graph has color-coded boxes side-by-side, indicating relationships.

For writers, the story line hangs like heavy cabling between power poles. Writers also use "cluster" or "bubbling" techniques to stimulate ideas and form stories. They start by jotting down an idea in a bubble, then scribble more ideas in secondary bubbles.

A secondary bubble may have its own set of bubbles, and so on. On paper, the end result is usually a sloppy page of roundish and overlapping shapes containing often misspelled words, yet in the mind of the author, the goal — big picture — is within vision.

In event planning, there is a time and place for the rigid structure of charts and graphs, but it's not in the beginning when creative juices are needed. It's at the end when you need to gather the results and present them in a manner that is understandable to those judging the success of your event.

OBJECTIVE

The word *objective* is that which pertains to an object; a purpose or goal; or a thing that can be seen or touched. A marketing plan attaches itself to the latter definition. What sets the objective apart from the goal is that it is not an obscure concept; it is accountable.

In building your plan, you must build in an accounting method for each of your objectives. For one objective, it is not unusual to include several checks-and-balances accounting systems.

If your objective is to sell 50 hot dogs, you can measure the sales by counting the hot dog tickets purchased, the monies received, and by counting the beginning and ending hot dog inventory.

Measurement of Results — at the beginning of your plan, be sure to identify what you intend to count, when the counting will occur, and what methods you will use.

STRATEGY

Strategy is a word often associated with military battles or the names of military heroes. When I think of strategy, I think of George C. Scott playing General Patton, standing in a jeep overlooking a battlefield, or James Mason as Rommel in *The*

Desert Fox, examining toy soldiers and tanks on the map in the war room.

Stars playing military heroes always seem to evoke a sense of "deep thinking." Strategists look at the situation from a historical perspective, examine it as it is today, then imagine how they want it to be in the future. After all this looking and thinking, they make a decision about the action they need to take. When you observe an event planner surveying an empty parking lot or venue during a site inspection, you may think you're watching a person stare at nothing, but the planner is mentally orchestrating what he wants to happen in the space.

TACTICS

When it comes to tactics, this is where the creative juices really start to flow. In Scrabble, it's like holding onto your "s" in wait for a word with a higher value.

Tactics are the implementation piece of the plan, the part of the plan that tells you what you have to put into motion to make the rest of it come together. *To celebrate the birthday, you need to invite the guests, bake or purchase a cake, put candles on the cake, and ask everyone to join in singing "Happy Birthday" as the birthday boy blows out the candles.*

Creating a solid event plan is about understanding the problem and finding a solution.

THE SIMPLIFIED EVENT PLAN

- Look at the big picture (goal).
- Establish what you want to accomplish (objective).
- Decide how you're going to attack the problem (strategy).
- Identify what you need to do to implement the plan (tactics).

...Then you focus on putting the wheels into motion

Understanding the company's mission statement and vision precede developing the event plan

---

The Event Plan

Goal: determine your overall mission — why you're doing this.

Objectives: quantify expectations — what you are going to measure and how.

Strategy: the method you'll use to attain your goal — the type of event.

Tactics: implementation — actions that need to be taken to activate your plan.

ANY EXCUSE FOR ~~A PARTY~~ AN EVENT

We want to have a party," whether said in a business or social environment, is a horrible reason to expend the effort required to produce an event. A fun-loving bunch of my friends referred to our group as the Fun Hogs of America. Our motto was, "Any excuse for a party." Having no excuse or reason is like losing the race before you set foot over the start line. To measure your success, you need a reason (or excuse) for your event.

	Milestone events	Other events
BUSINESS	Groundbreaking	Employee birthday
	Grand Opening	New contracts
	Anniversary	Annual meeting
	Expansion	Going-away parties
	New management	Awards ceremonies
	Public trading	Board meetings
PHILANTHROPIC	Capital campaign	Annual fundraiser
		Sponsor receptions
	Milestone events	**Other events**
FAMILY or SOCIAL	Birth	Birthdays
	Wedding, anniversary	Holidays, vacations
	Graduation	Celebration of life
CULTURAL or RELIGIOUS	Bris	Annual holidays
	Christening	Bar/Bat Mitzvah
	Quinceañera	

IDENTIFYING YOUR GOALS AND HIDDEN GOALS

Often, an event falls under the strategic or tactical portion of a corporate marketing plan. For the purposes of this book, we'll assume it has already been decided that an event will take place and your responsibility is to design and produce it. Keep in mind the terms *results-driven* and *measurement*. From beginning to end as you design the event, you must consider if your latest great idea will provide measurable results, as well as how and when they will be measured.

Start by asking yourself, "What is the underlying reason this event is taking place?" When you uncover the answer to that question, you'll be able to start identifying measurable objectives and start thinking about the style of the event.

Common answers to "Why are we having this event?"
- We always have it.
- The execs thought it would be good to boost morale.
- A party will attract more business.

Not-so-common answers (but often good excuses)
- At a local charity fundraiser, the president bought an auction item that included catering for 100.
- A famous musician said he'd do a concert for free.
- We need to get rid of all these leftover supplies.

HIDDEN GOAL

While you're searching for the main goal, you'll likely come across one or more *hidden goals*. A hidden goal takes refuge in a crack or cranny, where it finds solace in the background, watching the event evolve. Unless you find it in the early stages of planning, it can rear its ugly head after the event and scream, "Why didn't you pay attention to me?"

The answer your client or boss does not want to hear, or even sense, is, "I didn't know you (or your idea) were important."

You were paid, or you volunteered, to do this job. With the acceptance of that responsibility, you are always expected to be able to read the client's mind. Job title: event planner/producer/mind-reader.

A common mistake made by the novice event planner is to think about how the event looks before he understands why he is doing the event. The novice gets lost in thought about event night, the color of linens on the table, the catering staff in bistro aprons, and the long- stemmed flowers in glass vases. In the early planning stages, he should be focused on listening.

The art of listening takes us back to "keywords," the very first listing under Marketing Lingo. The boss may say his goal is publicity > which really means being covered by a radio station > which really means being covered by a radio station at drive time > which really means being interviewed by a specific talk show host > which really means a live interview by the host on a Thursday afternoon. When you identify the hidden goal, you are armed to cut to the chase and go after your target. Lengthy interviews on every radio show in town will not have the positive results impact of that one very short interview the boss really wants.

Now take a look at the same examples of answers from a deeper perspective. The deeper perspective will, more often than not, reveal the real reason for the event and help you identify your goal.

Common answers to "Why are we having this event?"

- We always have it.
    - ➡ Ever since the company opened its doors, we've held the family picnic.

        GOAL: to show our appreciation for our employees

            HIDDEN GOAL: to get the buy-in of family members

- The execs thought it would be good to boost morale.
    - ➡ The workforce has been reduced and those who are left are anxious because they think they're next.

        GOAL: to revitalize employees' attitudes and assure them of their position in the company

            HIDDEN GOAL: to retain the employees motivated to sell the product

- A party will attract more business.

    - ➡ All wrong — a "party" can backfire and attract only those who are available that night and time to eat free appetizers and drink wine. This party needs to be immediately turned into a marketing event.

        GOAL: to showcase the new product

HIDDEN GOAL: to show current clients and prospective customers the updated state-of-the-art warehouse

---

Understanding the goal and the hidden goal are the first steps to creating a successful results-driven event

---

Be wary of items offered for free or that are not a line item in your budget – servicing the item has a tendency to cost more than its value
Example: cupcakes and cookies are self-contained. A sheet cake needs to be cut and incurs the extra cost of plates, napkins, and forks

---

Not-so-common answers (but often good excuses)

- At a local charity fundraiser, the president bought an auction item that included catering for 100.

  ➤ *All right* — being fiscally responsible by sharing the expense of the upcoming employee recognition event using resources that came from benefitting a local charity, and eliminating a line item on the luncheon budget (assuming the luncheon was already planned and the food choice is a good match for the celebration luncheon).

  GOAL: use auction prize by the expiration date

  HIDDEN GOAL: to test the caterer's ability to work at the company's facility in advance of the company's upcoming week-long 20th anniversary open house

- A famous musician said he'd do a private concert for free.

  ➡ The boss wants to show off his college roommate, the now-famous musician, who has a tour concert scheduled nearby

  GOAL: invite employees and guests to the company facility, or board members to a private home for a free concert

  HIDDEN GOAL: the boss wants to invite and rub elbows with other local high-level executive friends of the musician, who could become new customers

- We need to get rid of all these leftover supplies.

  ➡ Donate the supplies to local charities that recycle

  GOAL: get the old branded collateral to the recycle bins on the ground floor without paying for labor — give the employees an hour off to carry the paper goods from their desk to the recycle area

  HIDDEN GOAL: educate the employees about recycling, and your favorite charity, by having the charity's representatives at your recycle drop-off point

You'll design the event around the GOAL, but satisfying the HIDDEN GOAL is what will really make you shine

MEASURING RESULTS

Objectives are the measureable piece of the event plan — the piece that holds the event planner accountable.

Objectives may be measured quantitatively and/or qualitatively. Measurement is the ultimate deciding factor in the success of the event and, as such, accurate measurement is key. Determine one or several methods of measurement for each objective.

Successful event producers prove their results by using pre-determined measurement techniques and reporting the results as facts: good, bad, or indifferent.

Measurement Terms

QUANTITATIVE: an amount or portion

New leads	Attendance	Retention	Sales
Dimension	Height	Volume (amount)	Brightness
Size	Weight	Volume (sound)	Cold
Extent	Length	Density	Heat
Capacity	Breadth	Speed	Variety
Recruitment	Depth	Strength	Duration

QUALITATIVE: a characteristic measurement

Good leads	Perception	Attitude	Potential
Upscale	Luxury	Formal	Compassion
Fashionable	Exotic	Nice	Clever
Pretty	Best	Funny	Sad
Spicy	Sweet	Charming	Happy

QUANTITATIVE and QUALITATIVE: *portions with characteristics*

Exposure	Back cover of the convention program; branded greeters at registration; product inclusion in swag bags; media coverage
Positioning	End cap in the grocery store; corner booth on trade show floor; room on executive level
Acceptance	Five seats at the private awards banquet; a presenter of an award; a guest speaker

METHOD: the process of taking the measurement

Survey	Research	Predict	Organize
Estimate	Observe	Fulfill	Count
Gauge	Analyze	Consult	Negotiate

TOOLS: equipment or means used to assist in process

Camera	Odometer	Graphics	Interviews
Compass	Speedometer	Tape recorder	Diagram
Caliper	Questionnaire	Video	Exit poll
Scale	Phone	Comment cards	Focus group

Use these examples as a springboard for your even measurements.
NOTE: The more specific you are in identifying your objectives,
the easier it will be to attain them

QUANTITATIVE

General	Specific	Hidden
Ticket sales	500	full price
Sponsorship	$10,000	cash only
Increased product sales	250 pieces	first-time buyers

QUALITATIVE

Happy guests	children	ages 0 — 5
Sponsor interest	in-kind	media
Attendee response	comment cards	parents

Need more ideas about what to measure? Here's an edited list of categories of customer satisfaction firms provided by the American Marketing Association.[1]

- Agency-Client Relationships
- Benchmarking
- Blueprinting
- Business-to-Business Customer Satisfaction Studies
- Company Image Studies
- Competitive Dissatisfaction
- Computer Analysis, Modeling, Processing, and/or Sorting of Customer Comments
- Consultative Assistance in Deployment
- Consumer Research
- Criterion-based Customer-Satisfaction and Pay-for-Performance Systems
- Customer Panel Development
- Customer Portfolio Analysis and Identification of the Decision-Making Process
- Customer Retention Research, Expectations Analysis, and Gap Profiling
- Customer Satisfaction; Employee Satisfaction Studies
- Customer Value Analysis
- Focus Group Facilities

---

1 Marketing News, October 28, 2002/a publication of the American Marketing Association; for current list of customer satisfaction categories see www.marketingpower.com

- Implementation/Training
- Integrated Voice of the Customer (VOC) System
- Internet and IVR Data Collection
- International/Global Customer Satisfaction Research
- Internet & E-mail Surveys
- Language Assessment (foreign)
- Lost Customer Research
- Quality Awards Assessments
- Market-Based Social Research
- Marketing Effectiveness
- Market Segmentation, Conjoint Analysis
- Measurement of Customer Feedback of Performance Over Time
- Measurement of Internal Customer Needs
- Mystery Shoppers
- On-Line Research
- Organizational Assessment
- Qualitative Identification of External Customer Needs & Satisfaction
- Quality Assessment of Vendors
- Quantified Measurement of External Customer Needs & Satisfaction
- Sales Staff Reviews
- Satisfaction and/or Service Evaluations
- Technology Research
- Telephone Data Collection
- Trade Research
- Web Research

SCHEDULING MEASUREMENT

Scheduling measurement is equally as important as deciding what to measure. Some items almost measure themselves, such as ticket sales and the amount of food consumed, which can both be measured with beginning and ending inventories.

What may be more important to the client is when the tickets are sold, whether they are sold ahead of time or on-site, and at what price level. At a day-long event, tracking the ticket count upon entry (throughout the day) will indicate the volume of people entering the event at a particular time.

Collecting tickets, hand clickers, and metered or electronic gates are tools used to gather ticket or attendance information. Color-coded or bar-coded tickets can indicate the price of the ticket and/or the sex or age (adult or child) — depending on the depth of information you desire and the amount of money you invest in creating and implementing the tracking system.

Create a schedule of times to measure, and make sure to provide staff with measuring instructions, tools, and a drop point for the measurement.

Hand stamps are often used to allow guests in-and-out privileges and eliminate double counting the same individual. Disposable colored wristbands serve the same purpose and may indicate age of the attendee when alcohol is served, or a VIP status for entry into restricted areas.

Besides use as an identification badge, ticket stubs, wrist bands, beverage cups, and 3-D glasses also provide an excellent space for sponsor branding, advertising, and coupons.

EVALUATING AND REPORTING

To accurately evaluate the quantitative results, during the planning stages you'll need to identify what you want to count, how you will count it, and when it will be counted. To accurately evaluate the qualitative results, the same process applies.

Both the planner and the boss (or company or client or committee — whoever has hired you or assigned you the project) need to agree on what will be counted, when it will be counted, and the method to be used.

Being in agreement and making use of predetermined measurement techniques will provide the straightforward guideline to judging success.

If the measurement has been scheduled and people have been assigned to do the measurement, at the end of the event you should have the desired raw data from which to document the results of the event and prove its success.

Reporting the results as facts is the only way to get an honest and accurate overview of the event. Eliminating a personal attachment to numbers makes it easier to understand how they relate to each other and the overall event.

Knowing the success factors expected, the event planner can design the event with results in mind.

SURVEYS

A good survey can be a valuable tool loaded with information otherwise not available. Survey questions should be considered seriously. You don't want too many, or too few, and they should pose a question that will supply the information the client really wants to know.

A survey of the attendees during the event will provide qualitative ("This is the coolest family event I've been to all year") and quantitative ("I brought all four children") information.

An on-site survey of the participants/vendors, if you have a festival or expo area, can provide information on their like or dislike of the site setup and their interaction with the attendees. These face-to-face participant surveys are valuable because the participants can provide feedback such as how many items they gave away or sold, if the audience was a good match for their products, and if they would consider returning to the event the next year.

In surveying the participants/vendors after the event, expect to receive fewer responses, as they are likely to be thinking of the next project on their calendar. A follow-up email thanking them for participating and asking for any comments gives them the opportunity to add additional remarks.

The vendors are usually surveyed after the event when they have their final counts. If you are interested in knowing what was sold at a particular time, be sure to ask your vendors to track sales by time, or assign someone to visit the vendor at a specific time to record sales numbers.

In preparing your post-event report (my company refers to this as the *Project Review*), be sure to include all suggested changes from the client, participants, vendors, guests, and event producers. This information can be used when planning next year's event and lessons learned can be applied to other events.

PROJECT REVIEW

The *Project Review* is a record of the event and includes items the planner and client have decided will be useful in documenting the event. It can be done as a PowerPoint, bound, loose-leaf, or binder document, or as a series of electronic files. Elements included are often also used in entries for awards competitions.

Project Review basic inclusions:
- Executive Summary
- Quantitative/qualitative measurement (graphs, charts, lists, photos)
- Media clippings and social media documentation
- Collateral, advertising, and promotion

Documentation — public view and private view

A well-presented Project Review is an excellent promotional tool. Depending on the end purpose of the documentation, often more than one version is created. Take care in setting aside documents intended only for private view, not public view.

Summary Recap

The smallest version will include enough visuals and factual information to interest the reader without boring him.

Production Review

For annual events, this piece serves as the blueprint for next year. A comprehensive package is comprised of all collateral materials created for the event, including materials for the vendors, participants, attendees, entertainment, committees, advertising, promotion, etc.

Confidential Review

Budgets, production schedules, contracts, sponsorship materials, site plans, and documents for private view should only be available to the client and planner.

NOTE: Recaps are included at the end of this first chapter for the purpose of bringing you back to the basics. The following three pages will serve as a summary of the process of designing and producing results-driven events. When you get lost in the process — return to these pages to get back on track.

RECAP: Elements of Your Event Plan

Executive Summary — one-page summary of findings

Mission Statement — who you are

Vision Statement — what you wish to become

Market Analysis — SWOT and Gap

Research Evaluation — summary of research information

Goals — identify your overall mission

Objectives — measurable quantitative and qualitative expectations

Strategy — the well-thought-out method to attain your goal

Tactics — implementation/action plan

SWOT and Gap Analyses — strengths/weaknesses, opportunities/threats, gaps

Needs Assessment — what is required to attain the objectives

Measurement of Results — how and when you intend to measure the effectiveness of the plan

Evaluation and Presentation — gathering, preparing, and submitting the results of the event in an easy-to-understand manner

Members of an integrated marketing team may include: Promotion, Human Resources, Operations, Administration, Sales, Facility, etc. The same department does not always take the lead, but they retain the same ultimate goal for their department as it relates to the project.

RECAP: Simplified Marketing Plan Outline

MISSION STATEMENT (what you do):

VISION (what you hope to become):

VALUES-CULTURE-INTEGRITY (fundamental beliefs and ethics):

GOAL (conceptual accomplishments — the big picture):

OBJECTIVES (measurable accomplishments) — The more specific you are in identifying your objectives, the easier it will be to attain them:

General objective
Specific objective
Hidden

STRATEGY (how you're going to accomplish the goal):

TACTICS (implementation) — what you're going to do to accomplish the objectives:

Each objective will have its own set of implementation tools.

#1 — Specific objective
      Steps   a)
                b)
                c)

RECAP: Measurement

MEASUREMENT (choosing a standard evaluation):

Quantitative
Qualitative

METHODS OF MEASUREMENT (deciding upon the most accurate way to measure the objective):

MEASUREMENT TOOLS (selecting from the variety of options available to record measurements):

SCHEDULING THE MEASUREMENT (establishing the best time to measure for accurate results):

Before
During
After

REPORTING — the Project Review (compiling and presenting the information in a manner that is understandable and best suits the audience for which it is intended):

UNDERSTANDING YOUR EVENT

Y ou can't get from point A to point B unless you know where you are, "A," and where you're going, the location of point "B." The same holds true in producing a successful event: you need to know the definition of success as it applies to your event — this can be accomplished through measurement. You also need to know and understand the key players — this is accomplished through their profiles.

It is also important understand the parameters within which you are working.

Here are some considerations as you build your event:
- Budget
- Venue location, date, day, time of day, duration
- Food and beverage
- Permits, security, insurance
- Publicity and promotion

The people piece of the event can include:
- Client or boss
- Committee

- Event staff (paid)
- Volunteers
- Jurisdictions
- Vendors and contractors
- Talent, entertainment, activities

When you start pulling the pieces of your event together, you'll find that research plays an important part in almost every aspect and in every decision you will make. As the elements fall into place, you'll see that one decision can impact the next and so on down the line.

Research and having the information at your fingertips is a valuable resource for the planner. Even after you have selected a vendor, keep information on your second choice readily available should the first choice be unable to provide the service you need.

During the research process, basic considerations are:
- Cost
- Experience (and references)
- Quality
- Ability to provide quantity
- Proximity to event site
- Availability

Research is a task that can be handed over to another person. If you plan to do so, be sure the person is asking the right questions and has enough of an understanding of the event that he is conscious of answers that may not be relevant at the particular moment.

For example, when researching and comparing costs of portable restroom companies, have the researcher make note if one company provides solar restrooms, showers, or executive trailers. Although they may not be listed as a line item in your budget today, if a sponsor insists on having solar restrooms, it's better to have that information where you can easily access it rather than having to research the topic a second time.

Take florists, for example: some carry silk trees; some don't — but during install you might find that you need them to fill in an empty corner of a tent or detract attention from an unsightly electrical box.

KNOW YOURSELF, KNOW YOUR PRODUCT

Odd as it may sound, you don't know your product, client, event, or even your own self as well as you think you might. A straightforward way to discover exactly what it is you're "selling" is to create a series of documents that will provide a good foundation for your project. Different organizations will call these documents by different names, often using the internal lingo of the organization. We'll refer to the information documents using the generic term *profile*.

You'll need information about the organization or client, the management or organizing committee, the sponsors, the workers (employees, volunteers, event staff), the vendors, site, honoree or benefitting charitable organization, and anyone else you can think of who is a "stakeholder" with a vested interest in your project. Getting this information upfront will serve as a solid foundation in designing the event as well as a body of reference material when you reach unexpected twists and turns in the road ahead.

Each stakeholder in your event has a reason for being involved and sometimes, a hidden agenda. Identify that reason and you'll be able to help him accomplish his goal, so that he can help you accomplish the event goal. It may be time-consuming to gather and review the information, but it will make your job easier in the end. Be sure to offer several delivery options (email, fax, hard copy) and request that the forms are delivered back to you by a specific date and time.

The more you know about the product, the people, and the purpose, the more likely you are to have a successful event.

COMMUNICATING WITH YOUR CLIENT

If your group of stakeholders is computer savvy and all are familiar with using on-line shared files and limited access or blocked information software, by all means use it. Educating stakeholders on new software has the potential to slow down, not speed up, your forward motion — not to mention the aggravation experienced by some when learning new software programs.

In addition to software programs, be wary of trying other methods of communication that might be new to your stakeholders, such as phone equipment or internet conferencing (like Skype), as the learning curve can focus the attention on the communications process rather than the gathering of information.

You'll need buy-in from the stakeholders on the communications tools to be used to share information and the expectation in using the tools. If you will communicate sometimes by phone at night or on the weekend, they should all agree to maintain access to their phone or be near a computer at those times.

It is also wise to set a policy that if a stakeholder is not available for communication, the rest of the group is notified or an alternate person substituted in the communications process.

It is important that the stakeholders know their input will be considered, but it must be received in a timely manner. Let everyone know you are moving forward in your design process by sending out an email to (or otherwise communicating with) ALL involved — something like, "Thanks to those of you who have responded by returning your completed forms; we'll start the event design process based on the information received."

WHO'S IN CHARGE?

The person in charge of the event may be referred to as the planner, coordinator, or any number of other titles indicating the person in charge. We'll refer to that person as the "director," and that person needs a profile, as do each of the participants on the planning team.

Planning Team Profiles:

At the onset of the project, individual profiles enable all involved to provide complete contact information as well as comments regarding their expectations — *what they expect to give to the project and what they expect to receive.*

As the director reviews these profiles, he is likely to see hidden capabilities of a particular individual that may work their way into the project. Johnny's profile reveals that he used to be a radio announcer. The director stores that information in the back of his mind, thinking Johnny would be a good alternative if the hired emcee is unable to attend at the last minute. Sue's profile reveals that she is a guest speaker at an overseas convention the day before the event. Although her participation in the planning stages is essential, from her profile the director knows not to schedule her with on-site responsibilities.

The director may be a paid employee of the company, a hired consultant, a retired professional volunteer, an inexperienced volunteer, or a person with any other range of event knowledge. The director's event know-how spans everything from design and production to the client's product, mission, and message. The director's range of knowledge is as broad as the background of the person selected as the director. With the speed of technology, some of his knowledge will be current, and maybe some dated.

The smart director identifies and employs the talents of the stake-holders and planning team

The Director Profile *(let's assume you are the director): includes basic contact information as well as a brief description of who you are today as you start this project.*

The director profile is not a résumé listing capabilities or history; you (the director) already have the job. Your profile is about you, the person — your personal likes and dislikes, and your expectations of the project.

At some time during the course of the planning, implementation, or post-event, it is likely that you will ask, "Why am I doing this?" Referring back to the director profile holds the answer to the question that will get you back on track. As the person in charge of the event, consider filling out the director profile as part of the project — you too may need time to reflect and in the profile, provide a good, solid answer to the question, "Why am I doing this?"

When you're at a loss for creative ideas, reviewing your own profile may also uncover an idea pertaining to your outside interests or personal goals for yourself through the event. At a loss for more activity ideas for your event? Say your profile shows that you restore cars — how about adding a static car display? Searching your memory bank can not only expand your perspective on the project, it can often lead to unusual and exciting solutions, and reinvigorate your interest.

Because of the complexity of events, it is easy for the director to get spread thin in addressing all the details. "If only I had just one thing to focus on instead of 1,000" or, "Why is this responsibility on my plate?" The answer to the second question is because you're in charge. The answer to the first is that you haven't yet identified that one special thing that will sustain your interest. You haven't identified your "signature" piece of the event. It is the desire to get your signature piece right that will motivate you through other, less glamorous phases of the production process. *Because of the strong connection between the director and the event, it is not unusual that the director's signature is also the event's signature.*

Identify the "one thing" that will personally bond you, the director, to the event.

Early in the planning stages, inject an element of special personal interest. It may be large, like fireworks or a parade; medium-size, like a presentation to a local organization or hosting a sponsor dinner; or small, like handwritten thank you notes or selecting the national anthem singer.

Your budget and conscience will guide you in finding your signature element. After you identify a grand idea, ask yourself:

- Will my idea enhance the event?
- Is it within budget?
- Can it be achieved in the given time frame?
- Do we have the resources available?
- Is there enough physical space at the site?

If the answer to all three is "yes," you have identified the one special element that forms an unbreakable bond connecting the director to the event. In a way, this bond is your personal "signature" on the event.

Example of a Director's Signature —
the Mascot Conga Line

In 2002, The Lundquist Company won the contract to design a family event celebrating the fifth anniversary of First 5 Sacramento, a county commission with the ultimate goal to enhance the health and early growth experiences of children, enabling them to be more successful in school and to give them a better opportunity to succeed in life.

After researching locations throughout Sacramento it was decided that the event would be held in Fairytale Town, a gated children's theme park located on the grounds of William Land Park, the largest public city park in Sacramento.

As the two venues are under separate management, one private with a board of directors and the other a city park, the event is actually two independent events taking place simultaneously and disguised as one big event. Each event venue has its own rules and regulations as well as separate permits, insurance, security, tenting, and furnishings. The gated part of the event houses the entertainment, food, and activities. The open park area is the site of the educational portion of the event.

In designing the event, I knew if it was successful, it could become an annual event. With 3,000 people in attendance in the first year, the Children's Celebration was successful and subsequent contracts for the event renewed. The original event design included moving the attendees from the free food and entertainment inside the Fairytale Town gates to the education expo outside the gates in the park. My solution was a conga line. Humpty Dumpty and Mother Goose (in costumes owned by Fairytale Town) would lead the conga line. I also invited some local mascots to participate. The simple logic was that the kids would see and follow the mascots, and the parents would follow the kids. The conga line would start at the stage and end in the Resource Expo located in the park.

After some official speeches from the stage, conga music blared from the loud speakers, the mascots came from behind the curtain, the kids ran to the larger-than-life characters, the parents followed the kids, and a tradition was born.

The Mascot Conga Line became the "signature element" of the Children's Celebration. Attendees and speakers alike participate — in 2011, California Congresswoman Doris Matsui joined Sacramento Supervisor Roger Dickinson (chairman of the First 5 Sacramento commission) as, after eight years of addressing the crowd and leading the conga line, he said his goodbyes to the crowd before taking the office of California Assemblyman, 9th District.

Supervisor Roger Dickinson (now Assemblyman Roger Dickinson), in his royal plastic crown and gold, gem-studded staff, led the Mascot Conga Line bobbing and weaving from the stage to the expo. In its eighth year, the event recorded more than 7,000 attendees and the Mascot Conga Line at its longest included 29 mascots and a marching band.

Each year, new elements are added to the First 5 Sacramento Children's Celebration, not only to keep it vibrant for the attendees, but to keep my mind actively thinking of new ways to entertain the crowd and myself.

The initial one-time event was so well-received, TLC was awarded the production contract through its 10th anniversary. The Children's Celebration has won local, regional, nationwide, and international awards, including an International Gala Award from *Special Events Magazine* for Best Festival in 2008 and 2011.

Did I mention I don't have kids? People ask how I can plan a children's event when I don't know anything about kids. The answer is that I know events and I know that identifying the elements that hold my signature guarantees my interest will be retained from conception to completion.

Owning the Title of Director

Since 2001, I have instructed the results-driven events class in the marketing certificate program at University of California Extension. The students range between 24 and 60 in age. There are people about to retire and people wishing to change careers. Their titles run the gamut from vice president of marketing to receptionist and even part-time staff. One thing is for certain: no one is immune from being assigned the temporary title of "event director."

On the first night of class I always ask the question, "Why are you here and what do you normally do?" Year after year, the answers are the same:

1. I'm in the marketing certificate program to increase my knowledge of marketing.
2. I'm looking for a career change
3. My boss assigned me the task of putting on an event for 500 people and I've never put on an event before.

My observation is that the boss (the decision-maker) often considers producing an event an easy job requiring little or no training. Actually, he doesn't even consider it "producing" but rather, just "doing." This nonchalant attitude about events couldn't be further from the truth, especially in a business setting.

All events in a business environment are marketing opportunities and should be given the attention and support of any other marketing activity.

To paraphrase Bruce Skinner, CFEE, and past president of the International Festival & Events Association, "Events are the one aspect of the marketing mix that put you in direct one-on-one contact with your audience."

I'll add a comment here that you should take to heart. Throughout the years and my interface with students, committees, my clients', staff, and my staff, across the board those who think they are expert at producing events because they have thrown a child's birthday party or the family picnic are the people who are the least likely to succeed at producing events, because they have a pre-determined idea of how to do something and are either unwilling to change or believe there is nothing to learn. It is the people who approach event design and production with the enthusiasm of a child at the zoo who have the greatest success.

What Makes the Director so Important?

I'm sure you've heard the phrase, "The buck stops here." Well, if you haven't been in the position of director before, let me assure you that phrase is accurate. Events unite a complex set of information and activities and require an attention to a broad range of details. Being an event director is like being mayor of a city, captain of a ship, or a high-ranking military officer.

As the director, you:
- Have a mission to accomplish
- Have activities to orchestrate
- Have people to manage
- Provide direction
- Make decisions
- Adjust plans
- Solve problems
- Manage budgets
- Oversee vendors
- Run meetings
- Interface with clients
- Work with volunteers
- Read contracts
- Order insurance
- Pull permits
- Dry people's tears and give pats on the back

Learn the information you really need to know by posing open-ended questions (who, what, when, where, why, and how) specifically relating to your expectations for your event.

After having read the list prior, develop the director profile questions. What would you like to know about the person you're hiring to lead the project?

Questions you might want to include regarding positions with past events and clients:

What types of decision-making powers have you had in the past?

Have you worked with volunteers, boards of directors, upper management, etc.?

Are you comfortable answering to your boss or client, or do you prefer to make decisions on your own without interference or comment from anyone?

Do you have firsthand experience working with vendors (selection, contract negotiations, on-site)?

Do you have the time and staff to support a project of this size and importance?

Do you fully understand the scope of the project?

Position with the event:

Can you afford to take a volunteer position?

Is the payment for your expertise adequate?

Are your shared responsibilities clearly defined?

Do you have personal connection with the event theme, benefactor, planning committee, etc.?

Why do you think this particular event important?

Do you have a plan to manage difficult situations?

Have you discussed this plan with the client?

Other comments (past event experience, hobbies or outside interests related to the event).

Misconceptions about the Event Director

Whether the event director is employed by the company, hired on a contract basis, or a volunteer, there is a general misconception that because there is an event director, he/she will ensure that the event runs successfully. I say this is a misconception because the title can lead stakeholders to believe that their input is unnecessary. This is most often seen when the expectations of both sides (director and stakeholders) are not clear. Stakeholder input is extremely important in designing and producing a successful event.

An event director is usually selected based on past performance, which often involves more than the individual. The company or organization can become disenchanted when they learn their new event director is not exactly what they expected because his capabilities don't translate well to the new position. Here are a few examples of what to look for when making your hiring decision. Also note the solutions to overcoming what may appear to be obstacles.

Before finalizing your interview questions s and/or the application form, have the questions reviewed by your human resources department to ensure they are in accordance with current employment laws.

PRIOR JOB	NEW JOB	NEW JOB SOLUTION
Had access to big-name sponsors	Signed an agreement with old boss not to solicit sponsorship from current in new position	Hire or mentor a sponsorship sales person

Created great graphics collateral	Graphics done by in-house graphic department at old job	Hire a graphic artist or offer an internship through a university
Understood budgets inside and out	Had an accountant who managed the numbers	This responsibility already managed by in-house bookkeeper
Excellent past experience with music events and annual corporate meetings	This is an athletic or arts organization, or a software designer, or food distributor	Basic event format and know-how translates from one arena to another

DIRECTOR PROFILE *(example)*

(On the form you design, insert the information you consider valuable to the success of your event — have your human resources department review your questions prior to distributing the form or conducting interviews)

Name	Nickname
Address	City/State/Zip
Home/office phone	Cell phone
Email	Website
Employer	Position
Family (position/responsibility)	
Outside interests (hobbies, social organizations)	

Short description regarding your personal goals and this particular event	
My goal	
My objectives	
1	
2	
My strategy	
My tactics	
1	
2	

Stakeholders — who are they?

Stakeholders come in all shapes and sizes and are different for every event. In large companies, which hold many events, the stakeholders are rarely identical from one event to another. Stakeholders can be any of the following

- Company management team or department
- Employees
- Employee family and friends
- Boards of directors
- Committee members
- Community representatives (nonprofit organizations and community-based organizations)
- Jurisdiction representatives (venues, governmental)
- Law enforcement and safety
- Participants (talent, entertainment, activities)
- Vendors (food, décor, staging, lighting, tents, sound, furnishings, HVAC, restrooms, floral)

What Do They Bring to the Table? Connections to People and Resources

Some capabilities are obvious, such as the accountant bringing accounting expertise. Some capabilities are not as obvious, such as the accountant building stage backdrops on the weekend because his brother is the local theater director and his nephew stars in a musical on Broadway. With this information we have now added access to stage craft, local talent, and a recognized star.

Connections to resources are equally important as they can be parlayed into reducing or eliminating budget line items. One resource that is often overlooked is the company graphics department, which often has a printing department. The company marketing and communications departments are also a great resource as they already have a team of professional public relations, marketing, and media people in place. And don't overlook the groups of employees available as on-site staff.

The Stakeholder Profile is also used to provide a foundation of information for the event and includes basic contact information. It differs from the director profile because it is important to understand the stakeholder's position with the company or organization.

Questions you might want to *carefully* phrase and include:

Position with their company:
- Do they have decision-making powers?
- Do they have the ear of a decision-maker?
- What is the title and responsibility in their company?

Position with the event:

- Are they paid or volunteer?
- What is their responsibility in the event?
- Are they on the executive planning committee?
- Are they on a subcommittee?
- Have they been involved in this event before?
- How have they been involved in this event before?
- Other comments (past event experience, hobbies or outside interests related to the event, etc).

You may want to use a different version of the same form for sponsors, vendors, committee members, and any other people or groups with a vested interest in your event.

➡ Ask appropriate questions of each group.
➡ Phrase open-ended questions.
➡ If an intermediary (such as a salesperson) will be collecting the information, ask that person to assist with phrasing the questions.

In addition to cash investments, you'll find that sponsors can be a valuable resource. The stakeholder profile is like a warm-up to the stakeholder's project profile in that it uncovers information about the stakeholder that can be beneficial as you design your event.

The information will be compiled into the project profile and will reveal the connections and resources the stakeholders bring to the table. The key is to identify the person who can provide the information or connections that would be helpful to the event.

If you want information, you need to know when the person with the information is most likely to be available to you and how he or she prefers to communicate

Making good use of a celebrity - a celebrity may be an entertainer or a person of stature in your organization or known to your audience.

Celebrities are mentioned here because stakeholders often have the connections. If the celebrity agrees to lend their name or face to your event, think of how they might be involved before, during and after. Although a live performance would be great, they don't have to physically be at your event to impact its success.

A pre-event email, voicemail, or tweet from this person to your target audience can excite your audience and positively impact the receipt of your message and the attendance at your event. Think of what they might have to offer such as autographed merchandise, tickets, and connections to other celebrities.

STAKEHOLDER PROFILE (example)	
(On the form you design, insert the information you consider valuable to the success of your event — have your human resources department review your questions prior to distributing the form or conducting interviews)	
Name	Nickname
Address	City/State/Zip
Home/office phone	Cell phone
Email	Website
Employer	Position
Best time to reach you	
Preferred means of communication	

Role or responsibility in the event
Experience in event role
Other (past experience, hobbies/outside interests related to this event)

Be sure to allow adequate time to review the provided profiles and remember to read between the lines. Some-one who has done the same job in the event for 20 years can still be doing it because he a) is very good, b) is hor-rible at it but no one has the nerve to replace him or her, c) has a bad attitude and wants to get out of it, but it's a lousy job and no one will take it, or d) just likes to be in-volved and has been flying below the radar, which might warrant a special commendation.

The Project Profile is used to provide additional information used during the event design process.

"Section One: Marketing" provided the blueprint for de-veloping the results-driven event plan.

You already have the stakeholder profile; now you want to know what each stakeholder thinks about the project — his vision of the event, and what he personally expects it to accomplish. To ensure your stakeholders understand what you are asking of them, ask for specific and general answers to questions.

The Project Profile:
- Is filled out by the stakeholders
- Enables the director to design a results-driven event using the information of importance to the stakeholders
- Reveals gaps in the project

The project profile shows how closely the committee is aligned with the overall vision and purpose of the event. The information requested should include specific goals, objectives, and expectations of each of the stakeholders. This is another source of hidden agendas. Not that the stakeholders are purposely hiding something from you, but rather that they may have forgotten to tell you, or they assume you already know.

Why Create a Project Profile:
- Get everyone on the same page.
- Adjustments, major or minor, at this stage are far easier to manage than after the implementation is already in motion.
- As the project profile is anonymous, it gives all stakeholders the opportunity to speak their two cents' worth without fear of being criticized.

PROJECT PROFILE (example)
This is an anonymous form. Your identification will not be disclosed at any time.
On the form you design, insert the information you consider valuable to your event

#1   Target audience YOU would like to reach
 	
        Example:
 	
                General — new homeowners
 	
                Specific — Chamber of Commerce board members

#2   Goals YOU would like to see achieved through a series of events
 	
        Example:
 	
                General — media coverage
 	
                Specific — newspaper articles in a 50 mile radius

#3   Goals YOU would like to see achieved through a particular event
 	
        Example:
 	
                General — celebrate the completion of the project
 	
                Specific — formal gala dinner — showcase the project designer and implementation team
 	
Other comments

Final submission date is ____ at ____ via fax, mail, email. *Questions — call _____ at _____ or email _____*

When posing questions, be sure to ask specific questions. "Invite the city council members" is different from "Invite the city council members of the five surrounding cities."

Building a plan to record results is based on agreed-upon expectations. The expectations are documented in the information provided by the stakeholders. If a specific desire is not identified by a stakeholder, it cannot be accomplished. The clearer the stakeholders' response to their expectation, the easier it will be to identify a measurable objective and the appropriate measurement technique.

GLEANING INFORMATION FROM THE PROJECT PROFILES

When the project profiles are returned to you, prepare an anonymous spreadsheet with the answers to the questions. It is not necessary to associate names with responses; it is more important that you have recorded all requests.

The spreadsheet format works well for presenting information in an unemotional manner, and the committee will easily be able to identify the answers to incorporate into the event.

After the information is compiled and reviewed, you'll end up with two things:

A spreadsheet to be reviewed by the committee

A checklist indicating the agreed upon line items to be incorporated into the event.

From here you build the results-driven plan.

Depending on your questions, you might also uncover information that will be valuable in developing the plan. Here's a mini-example of a project profile answers spreadsheet. The third answer to question #5 was submitted by the CFO, who was unable to attend any pre-planning meetings, but had a vested interest in the project. Had it not been for his comment regarding alcohol, this event could have had disastrous results. Because of his comments, we were able to adhere to a tropical theme and create colorful non-alcoholic drinks.

Send the project profile form to people who may not attend meetings, but who are stakeholders — their input is important both in the event design stage and when reviewing your results.

Question #2: When should the event be held — day and time?	
2	Wednesday after work
2	Thursday 4:30 p.m. — 7:30 p.m.
2	Early evening during the week
2	Not on Monday (company softball; not on Tuesday (City Council meeting)

Question #5: What beverage would you like to see served?	
5	Self-serve keg beer, wine, lemonade — no ice tea
5	Bottled beer and wine form local vineyards
5	Our by-laws state we can't serve any alcohol
5	Full bar with professional bartenders

The project profile gives the stakeholder the opportunity to voice his opinion and have it recorded. The committee will consider every comment and identify those to use. This is a good place to find out who the stakeholders expect to be invited, and who they believe should be included in the program and how (e.g., speaking, printing programs, being acknowledged from the stage, etc.).

The project profile is the perfect vehicle to identify connections that can be beneficial to the success of your event. Remember, everybody talks — the owners, employees, vendors, contractors, spouses, friends, and other business associates — especially about something as important as a groundbreaking, grand opening, anniversary, name change, product launch, or any other celebration.

The key people involved in your upcoming event have already discussed it with their contacts, many of whom have shown an interest in being involved. The trick here is to remind your key players of these discussions by asking who they've talked to and what the people said in response.

Resources: List the individuals or companies who HAVE ALREADY DISCUSSED WITH YOU their interest in participating.

Also note if the conversation was general or specific.

Example:

General — food (the local chain restaurant)
Specific — printing (the copy center — donating 1,000 photocopies)

Individuals or companies LIKELY to participate and how

- Business contacts with a vested interest in your project: current vendors, contractors, bankers, security, suppliers, investors

- Personal contacts: social, religious, or political contacts

DEVELOPING STRATEGIES TO REACH YOUR TARGET AUDIENCE

There are multiple marketing techniques and tools that can be used individually or combined to make your marketing effort successful. Knowing your product and your audience will help you determine which techniques to employ. Although it's tempting to try something that hasn't been done before, start with the basics you know will provide results, then add the creativity.

RELATIONSHIP MARKETING

Relations marketing is a marketing approach with focus on the customer, i.e., your audience.

The purpose is to build and maintain a solid and positive connection between the customer and the product. To this end, knowing your audience gives you an advantage. Knowing all about your audience gives you an even bigger advantage. The more research you do to create an in-depth profile of your audience, the more likely you are to touch them and retain their following.

The primary reason to identify our audience after thinking about your goals, objectives, strategies, and tactics is that you are likely to let your mind wander and discover an audience you had not before considered.

All products and services have an audience that is relatively easy to identify — most people with feet wear shoes. But it's the target audience that already love your product (even though they may not have met your product yet) who will make a faster purchasing decision. Why? Because the product offers a solution to their specific need or problem. It's not just a running shoe — it's a running shoe for long-distance runners with narrow feet, or it's a dressy, wide-width flat-heel shoe for the woman recovering from foot surgery who has to attend a formal event and wants to look stylish.

Sales efforts meet the needs of the product.
Marketing efforts meet the needs of the audience

A successful event mirrors its audience.

Results-driven events are successful because they serve their audience.

They're designed to:
- Showcase the product
- Accomplish defined goals
- Show measurable results

Using an event as a marketing tool means, first and foremost, that the event must be attractive to the audience you desire. Year after year, when I run into former students of mine, this is the one comment they repeat back to me, as if it changed their entire perspective on events, and became their secret guide to using events as marketing tools. It's so pivotal that I'll repeat it again:

A successful event mirrors its audience.

FINDING YOUR AUDIENCE

Grasping the concept that you have to do research to identify your audience is both obvious and not so obvious. Your audience may "look" like one type of person and actually be another type of person or several other types of people. Besides how people look, you may want to consider how they think, how they live, their peer group, income, zip code, work status, etc.

People are ever-changing. Human nature causes us to always be reaching for something new, and as soon as we find it, we reach for something else. You must stimulate, sustain, and revitalize your brand to keep your current clients/audience, and to develop new ones.

Research helps you profile your target client.

Primary Research (a.k.a. field research) — developed for a specific client by interacting with his audience, i.e., phone polls.

Secondary Research (a.k.a. desk research) — third-party research studies regarding the market you wish to attract, i.e., census, tourism, local chamber, and business reports.

Qualitative Research — opinions, attitudes, and perceptions.
A qualitative questionnaire asks general to specific questions to reveal a cause of action.

    Why do you drink ___ soda?
    What would make you drink more _____soda?

Quantitative Research — measurement, numbers.
A quantitative questionnaire asks general to specific close-ended questions. (Avoid questions with yes or no answers.)

What kind of soda do you drink?

How many _____ do you drink daily?

Observational Research— look at your clients to learn what they're wearing, driving, eating, talking about, doing in their leisure time, etc.

Market Intelligence: Knowledge of how the external environment relates to your audience.

- Social - what do they do
- Economic - how much money to they make
- Psychographic - what are they thinking
- Demographic - age, gender, occupation, zip code, income
- Geographic - where they live
- Forecasting - what the market will want next
- Customer satisfaction - have their expectations been met?

Competitive Intelligence: What is the competition doing and is it working?

Life Cycle: Motivation, interests, and habits change as people age. When designing events for targeted age groups, think about how, where, and with whom they spend their time.

Lifestyle: Age groups can be further targeted by their basic life interests and choice of living style, such as students, ranchers, people with vacation homes, etc.

Environmental signals: Indications of what's happening now.

- Trends - fashion, music, color, hair cuts
- Causes or issues - recycle, save the whales

- Consumer behavior - take-out food, shop on-line
- Herd behavior - following something popular with like-minded people

---

An audience is a moving target. I'll say it again louder so you re-member: An *audience is a moving target.*

In 2010, Mitch Dorger, past CEO of the Pasadena Tournament of Roses (a.k.a. Rose Parade) was the keynote speaker at the California Festivals & Events (CalFest) Convention in Anaheim. He referenced a quote by Alvin Toffler in his book Future Shock[2], "Nothing is more dangerous than yesterday's success," which is similar to a comment made by a favorite doctor friend of mine, "What have you done for me lately?" I mention this here to reinforce that the audience is a moving target. What attracts a parent today will not attract a parent ten years from now, or even two years from now. The seniors of today will respond differently than the seniors before or after them.

---

*Always believe your event may have a possibility of being annual —
stash more ideas in your planning box than you'll actually use.*

As proven by internet marketing geniuses like Amazon and Facebook, after you sign up on an internet site, it is likely that you will receive information of specific interest to you. My local grocery store, office supply store, and pharmacy send me offers all the time about things I really do care about. At first I wondered, "How do they know?" The answer is that their advanced software tracks your in-store and on-line purchases, then match-

---

[2] Future Shock, Alvin Toffler, 1970, Putnam

es them to like purchases by other buyers, or similar products, and suggests other items that might interest you.

If you have the capability of capturing information from your audience, you have the beginning of your own research database. Lists of zip codes divided by economic status have long been available. If you have a specific profile of the kind of person you wish to find, there is a good chance you can purchase a list of people that match your criteria.

Beware of using unauthorized lists from private clubs or organizations

---

When looking for new audiences, the areas I personally find most interesting to consider are life-cycle, lifestyle, and environmental signals. Lists for the obvious groups and zip codes can be easily purchased. Finding the hidden audience is like a game with a high-stakes potential for results.

A reliable list of people in your market can fizzle out as life cycle changes alter their spending and entertainment habits. For instance, a sold-out "primer to great musical works" symphony concert that used to be attended by 20 to 30-year-olds has gone flat. The females have probably traded in peep-toe pumps for sneakers and carpools, while the males redirected their entertainment allotment to a home theater, and buying children's video games. Ticket sales probably plummeted because a new younger audience was not nurtured and the older audience outgrew the musical selections.

Finding the younger audience to educate means searching lists for college grads and young professionals. But what about the audience that used to be those new college grads and young professionals? They've already taken the symphony primer; now you have to figure out how to reignite their interest. This is where we start looking at what makes people tick, rather than the results (zip codes, cars, houses).

In the case of the used-to-be younger symphony audience, perhaps an even child-centered interpretation of favorite classical tunes will entice them to bring their children to an afternoon in an orchestra hall. Classical music is touted as intellectual food for developing brains. Pregnant women are listening to symphonic classics, and there are versions of the old maestros for babies. Recently I saw a crib with a built-in music box that played standard lullabies as well as Pachelbel's Canon. Look to social trends to find a way to reinterpret your offering for a different market or life cycle.

Life Cycle: Motivation, interests, and habits change as people age.

When designing events for targeted age groups, think about how, where, and with whom they spend their time. To reach a senior, you might want to create a family event or an interactive grandparent/grandchild event that specifically skips a generation. Cookie-baking, kite-making, collecting sea shells, building bird houses, and fishing are all activities that connect older folks to younger folks. Staging a car wash takes togetherness a step further by offering the opportunity to teach the youngsters about community service.

Interested in reaching teenagers? You're no longer limited to checking out church groups, organized sports, and fraternal clubs. Today's youth take horseback riding lessons and dance classes. They cruise the shopping malls, and prepare to compete in professional sports. The Internet greatly increases your chances of identifying a particular teenage interest in your community.

Lifestyle: Age groups can be further targeted by their basic life interests and choice of living style, such as students, ranchers, people with vacation homes, etc.

Urban living enables all ages to live in the midst of an active environment with restaurants, shopping, movie theaters, and nightlife within easy walking distance. Resort-themed neighborhoods with pools and event centers, and environmentally friendly neighborhoods with walking paths and parks, also indicate particular lifestyle preferences.

People with vacation homes or people who enjoy cruising can be in different age groups, but relate due to mutual interests. A group can also be targeted by age, then further narrowed down by interest.

ENVIRONMENTAL SIGNALS

Trends — fashion, music, color, haircuts

Trends are actions or activities copied by individuals that become a grouping of people doing or acting in the same way.

Trends are relatively short-lived, most visible in the fashion scene, and usually associated with an age group.

Television shows can create trendy looks for young viewers, such as necklaces with your name on them in *Sex and the City*, as easily as for older viewers, as with caftans in *The Golden Girls*. Everything from bowling shirts to sweat pants, holiday sweaters to stiletto heels, has become trendy through the power of television.

Causes or issues — recycle, save the whales

Watch the news and when you see a cause-oriented segment, you'll often see a variety of age groups represented. From environmentalists to health care reform, supporters of causes in all shapes, sizes, and age groups come together in support of an issue. The bonus here is that you can use multiple forms of communication to get your point across to the variety of audiences.

Consumer behavior — take-out food, shop on-line

Latching onto a specific consumer behavior or, better yet, being at the forefront of a movement or including a consumer behavior in your event plan can give you an edge up on the success of your event.

Communicating via the Internet and texting has quickly become the societal standard. Event marketing should cater to the techno-savvy market. Emails to targeted audiences announce events, while tweeting during an event can move a crowd from one location to another.

Even old-school audiences with limited technology capabilities are finding ways to access information about things of particular interest to them. Not that many years ago, it was news when Sunday church services could be seen on television; now churches post excerpts of sermons on their web sites.

Herd behavior — following something popular with like-minded people.

"Everybody's doing it" is a retailer's dream — from tanning salons and 60-minute chair massages to ordering fresh, locally grown produce and movie tickets on-line. It doesn't take a lot of people to agree the idea is valid; it takes a strong leader with lots of followers. Sweatshirts have had hoods for more than 50 years, but more recently they're worn over the head as a fashion statement. Now you can even design your own hoodie.

ENTICING THEM TO COME — HOW WILL THEY BENEFIT?

"Build it, and they will come" is a fine dream, but in today's climate of ongoing competition for audiences, just building it usually won't attract the size or quality of audience you want. In keeping with identifying your target audience or audiences, you need to entice them to come by letting them know how they will benefit.

Marketing lessons teach us to think about the steak and the sizzle. Is it the meat or the description of the meat that actually attracts the diner? The feature is that the button is red in color; the benefit is that when you push it, it makes a buzzing sound.

In designing your event, consider what will entice your potential audience into attending. Here are some basic examples:

- Free food and beverage
- Entertainment and activities
- Networking with business people
- Rubbing elbows with celebrities and politicians
- Swag bag
- Valet parking
- VIP seating, private party, behind-the-scenes
- Opportunity to see a venue for the first time
- Premiere, preview, or product launch

Remember the steak and the sizzle. The feature is the red button and the benefit is the sound it makes when you push it.

FEATURES	BENEFITS
Inclusive ticket price	No need to bring extra cash
On-site parking	Easy access to venue
Shotgun start	Everyone finishes at the same time

On-site covered parking	No umbrella needed
Five stages	Better chance to get close up
Beer and wine bar	Multiple choice

GIVING YOUR EVENT "LEGS": DELIVER YOUR MESSAGE BEFORE, DURING, AND AFTER

One indication of a savvy event designer is that he or she is aware of the vast marketing opportunities available using an event as a marketing tool. Whether you are staging a public or in-house company event, you can give your event legs by delivering your message before, during, and after the actual event.

Why would you want to do this? Because the repetition of your message is often what makes it stick in the minds of your audience members. Whether you're trying to influence their behavior (buy your product or be more productive), provide information (nonprofit mission or product launch), or thank them (recognition dinners or corporate picnic), the more chances you have to deliver your message the more likely the audience is to grasp and respond to it.

Delivering your message before, during, and after also opens the doors to endless opportunities such as:

Testing delivery methods: email, voice mail, regular mail, posters, flyers, paycheck inserts, display ads, radio, television, internet web site, social media

Targeting different markets for the same event: employees, families, the general public, special interest groups

Showcasing sponsors: logos, links to web sites, attract new sponsors

Involving departments: focus on particular employees or programs within the organization or business

Although in the initial planning stages identifying your target audiences and their preferred means of communicating can seem tedious, you will have a higher rate of success because you will be speaking to them in a language they understand.

Communications examples:

BEFORE: email, voice mail, regular mail, posters, flyers, paycheck inserts, print display ads, radio, television, internet/ web site, bus benches, traditional paper billboards, electronic freeway billboards, links to sponsors' and partners' web sites, internet advertising, mixers with sponsors and event team, social media

DURING: informational and directional signage, day-of schedules, programs, announcements from stage, washable tattoos, social media, promotional giveaways, photos with celebrity guests

AFTER: post event thank you using any or all of the above mentioned techniques, photo documentation of the event showing the sponsor/partner participation. Note: photo documentation can also be used to solicit sponsors for the coming year. Be sure to have proper release forms signed by the persons in the photographs if you intend to use photographs for commercial marketing purposes.

YOU'RE EXPECTED TO BE CREATIVE — WE WANT TO SEE RESULTS

We have all learned lessons, and often best remember those that are simple and straightforward. Laurie Heller has worked with arts organizations in Sacramento for the 20 years I've known her. She is one of the smartest people I know. We met when I was contracted to work on an event for the local PBS station, and we continued to work together on projects after she left the station.

When Laurie worked with the Sacramento Metropolitan Arts Commission, I was contracted to assist on several events. During one meeting, after I presented an idea that I honestly believed was brilliant (because of course, it was), Laurie's response was simply, "You're expected to be creative — we want to see results."

I can pinpoint Laurie's comment as the turning point in how I approached events. "How obvious," I thought. Of course they expected me to be creative; after all, creativity — along with my event design and production skills — is why they hired me. Whether you were randomly assigned the task, or have years of specific education, when you accept the title of event planner, it is assumed that you are both detail-oriented and creative. Add to this mix some marketing know-how, and you will easily be able to provide your client extensive information on his audience, or whatever other results he expects to gain from the event.

MEASUREMENT

Although I had always considered tracking the number of tickets sold to be part of the basic preparation process, it wasn't until this time that I embraced the mission of recording anything and everything that could be measured. Measurement became my secret weapon that provided my clients with a hefty arsenal of intelligence about their audiences.

Measurement is also a secret ingredient in keeping sponsors happy. In the same way that you determined what your client might wish to have measured, apply that logic to your sponsors and partners. You have already identified your potential sponsors and partners and while doing so, created profiles on them either as individuals or businesses. On their sponsor profile, ask that they comment on their expectations when participating in your event or any event they sponsor. These answers will guide you in identifying something to measure.

As a sponsor, one of the benefits in the sponsorship agreement might be to measure something of specific interest to the sponsor. Alternatively, measurement might be an added value offered to the sponsor that is not formally written into the agreement.

In addition to numbers like overall attendance and the general audience profile, here are some examples of measurables that might be of interest to a sponsor:

- Venues (entertainment or activities) with the largest audiences
- Record of time (audience size and profile)
- Sponsor product distribution or sampling (peak times and quantity)
- Breakdown of attendance (ratio of children to adults)
- Parking lot activity (indicates turn of the crowd)
- Types of vehicles in the parking lot

Once you have identified a new means of measurement, look to the future and find something else to measure.

HEAD COUNT — MEASUREMENT EXAMPLE

Numbers documented below confirm that at least 3,200 people attended.

BODY COUNT: SOURCE OF PEOPLE	PEOPLE ON-SITE	NO BAND or ID
Guest per venue "clicker" count 10am - 2pm	3,193	0
Venue volunteers	17	17
Venue staff	8	8
The Lundquist Company (event staff)	10	0
Audio/visual company	3	3
PR company	2	2

Media	4	4
Talent (emcee, entertainers, speakers)	9	9
Mascot & handlers	12	12
Catering	6	6
Client staff	6	0
Client volunteers	6	0
Hands-on's (fire dept, police, etc.)	14	14
Vehicles (library, smile, other)	5	5
Contractors (est. 2 per table)	<u>50</u>	<u>50</u>
TOTAL ATTENDING	**3,345**	**130**
<u>BAND COUNT</u>		
Wrist bands - kids (yellow)	1,458	
Wristbands - adult (blue)	1,293	
Estimate 10% unbanded	319	
TOTAL BANDED	3,070	
<u>COMPARISON COUNT</u>		
Venue COUNT	3,193	
Wristband COUNT	3,070	
Double count, talent, contractors, hands-on, etc.	123	

FOOD COUNT
Venue: Food for 3,000 (served noon - 1:30pm)
Resource expo: 120 snack bags provided to contractors, talent, hands-on, etc.
Water: 3,000 bottles ordered; 1,440 left over and taken to shelter
Client: 1,500 goodie bags, 105 English promotional items, 85 Spanish promotional items. All English distributed; 1,000 coupons with 1(800) number given out to order more promotional kits; 1,500 complimentary bus passes.

MEASURING BY THE SENSES

The more senses that are aroused by any event element, the more possibilities there are for measurement

	SEE	HEAR	FEEL	TASTE	SMELL
SENSE →					
ELEMENT ↓					
Popcorn	●	●	●	●	●
Fireworks	●	●	●		●
Parade	●	●	●		●
Car race	●	●	●		●
Auction & auction items	●	●	●	●	●

The Five-Point Quick Reference Guide
For MEASURING RESULTS

RESULTS:

Successful event producers prove their results by
using predetermined measurement techniques and
a wide variety of documentation methods.

1)   Identify measurable objectives and define means of
measurement.

       Quantitative objectives:

       Qualitative objectives:

       Hidden objectives:

2)   Determine one <u>or more</u> measurement tools.

3)   Develop a plan (and a back-up plan) for gathering source
material and recording the results.

4)   Report the results as facts, whether good, bad, or indifferent. Include suggested changes from client, vendors, guests,
event producers. Collate and summarize the results.

5)   Provide your client with a professional looking summary
document, and be prepared to supply original source material (if requested). Include copies of support collateral

Measurement as a key element is being able to boost your bottom line results. There is no limit to what can be counted. However, you need someone to count it. Depending on how specific the count, this is often a good job for a volunteer. If the measurement element is included in the benefits package, a paid staff person should be in charge of collecting the information.

Measurement reminders:
- Identify exactly what is to be counted.
- Provide an example of how it is to be counted.
- Schedule the time or times for counting.
- Schedule the personnel to do the count.
- Assign a responsible person to oversee the counters.
- Place counted documentation in a safe location.
- Record calculation as soon as possible.
- Review calculations and make assessment of the numbers.
- Provide sponsors and partners with easy-to-read and professional documentation.

PHOTOS:

Something sponsors seldom ask to have is a visual record of their on-site presence. Measurement photos can easily be taken of their booth, banners, interaction with audience, etc. Alert your photographers to also capture photos of problem areas, such as overflowing garbage cans and tripping hazards, so that these issues can be reviewed and corrected for the next event.

BUILDING THE RIGHT EVENT TO ACCOMPLISH YOUR GOALS

Repetitive as it might seem, it's time to think back to the initial concept of developing a marketing plan or event plan for your project. After reading the section on measurement, you probably have some great ideas on what can be measured and how you can do the measurement. Now the question is: are you measuring the right thing? Also, will this measurement be of interest to your client?

Look back at your event plan or use the sample on the opposite page to confirm that you're on track. Referring to this simplified plan often throughout the planning stages will help you adhere to the agreed-upon plan, and set the stage for gathering measurements.

Keeping your focus on the audience and the agreed-upon event plan is the best advice I can give both a novice and experienced planner. Too many times I've seen a great idea implemented that not only requires unbudgeted dollars or staff time, but is also inappropriate for the event.

Referring back to the agreed-upon event plan can assist you in staving off suggestions by your client, boss, or committee that don't add value to the plan. Use it as a safety net and road map when you feel the event is taking a wrong turn, and BEWARE of suggestions that come from persons in power if you see the ideas are not on track with identified goals.

(SIMPLIFIED)
MARKETING/EVENT PLAN OUTLINE

The foundation of your organization's or client's business.

GOAL (conceptual accomplishments — the big picture):

OBJECTIVES (measureable accomplishments): The more specific you are in identifying your objectives — the easier it will be to attain them.

> General objective
>
> Specific objective

STRATEGY (how you're going to accomplish the goal)

TACTICS (implementation) what you're going to do to accomplish the objectives. Each objective will have its own set of implementation tools.

> #1 Specific objective
>
> Steps   a)
>
>   b)
>
> #2 Specific objective
>
> Steps   a)
>
>   b)
>
> #3 Specific objective
>
>   a)
>
>   b)

RESULTS: Prove the results by using the predetermined measurement techniques. Report the results accurately (from the client's, vendors', guests', event producer's) provided facts. Include suggested changes.

ENHANCING THE PROJECT THROUGH THE RIGHT SUPPORT PROGRAMS

The active creative mind can dream up unlimited numbers of ideas and themes for events. Just look around your own business or social life. It won't take long to recall an event that seemed to have no purpose; nothing, other than spending time, was accomplished, and you left wondering why you had attended.

This situation occurs because the planner was more interested in the look and theme of the event than the reason the event was taking place or the guest experience. Whether a business or social event, the planner is easily mesmerized by the choices of rental linens and tabletop possibilities, not to mention the floral, props, and warehouses of décor. You see this often with a novice planner, a non-planner who is assigned to the task because there is no one else to do it, or a committee planning an event together.

Purpose and theme — don't plan an event for the purpose of throwing a theme party. Identify a purpose and design the event theme to enhance the purpose

The visual element of an event can easily preoccupy the planner to the point that he or she completely misses the ingredients needed to make the event a success. A fancy decorated ballroom by itself has limited staying appeal. After the initial *oohs* and *aahs*, the guest is ready for the next experience. If the food and entertainment feel like an afterthought to the décor, the guest experience will be disappointing.

Even if the purpose of your event is as simple as providing a distraction, a few hours for employees to get away from their desks, you can create a meaningful event that is both measurable and memorable. Time is something that can't be replaced, so as you plan your event, make sure to think about providing engaging value to the attendees.

Keep your focus on your audience — valet parking and a swag bag may be exciting to one group and expected by another.

SPONSORSHIPS AND PARTNERSHIPS

There are many good reasons to develop sponsorship and partnership opportunities as you design your event plan. Both sponsorships and partnerships are agreements between the company or organization staging the event and other businesses, organizations, or individuals with an investment in the event. In exchange for benefits associated with the event, the investment can be financial or in the form of traded goods and services.

Over the years, the event industry has used the terms *sponsorship* and *partnership* interchangeably. More recently, sponsors are referred to as partners — I believe to make the business relationship feel more like a personal relationship. As there is a distinct difference between the exchange of money and the exchange of goods or services, I choose to distinguish investments in an event as either a sponsorship or a partnership with the following definitions.

Sponsorship is an agreement to support an event, activity, person, or organization financially in exchange for benefits as outlined in the sponsorship agreement.

Partnership is an agreement to support an event, activity, person, or organization through an in-kind donation of products or services in exchange for benefits as outlined in the partnership agreement.

My differentiator is whether the investor is giving cold hard cash, which I use to purchase goods and services needed to produce the event, or whether the investment is goods and services. Although goods and services can be bartered to acquire other products, they can be as beneficial as they can be troublesome.

It is not unusual that a sponsorship agreement (cash) will include the opportunity for the sponsor to showcase his product on-site with a display or give-aways, or involve his employees as event staff. This is a good mix of cash backed with goods and services.

Sponsorship opportunities (examples)

- Title sponsor — name included in the title of the event
- Venue sponsor — name posted at the venue (stage, beer garden)
- Activity sponsor — pie-eating contest, race, face painting
- Talent sponsor — headline or walk-around talent
- Food — attendee food court, sponsor's reception, on-site VIP area
- Beverage — alcoholic and nonalcoholic (water, coffee, wine)
- Transportation sponsor — loaner vehicles or airline tickets
- Lodging sponsor — sleeping rooms
- Parade sponsor — costumed characters, media
- Special event (within the event) — special concert or speaker
- Ticket or backstage sponsor — tickets and passes
- Print — all event collateral

- Rental — tents, furnishings, tables, chairs
- Uniforms — logo event attire

Sponsorship Benefits (examples)

- Brand visibility
- Pre-event and on-site
- Display ads
- Signage
- Print collateral
- Staffing a booth
- Providing emcee or talent
- Samplings or product giveaways
- Signage
- Banners
- Informational and directional signs
- Flyers
- Maps
- Day-of programs
- Pre-event promotional posters
- Commemorative posters
- Autograph signing of commemorative posters
- Reaching your target audience one-on-one
- Networking with other sponsors
- Employee involvement in community activity
- Support a worthy cause

LEVERAGE SPONSOR OPPORTUNITIES

Look beyond the cash for the real sponsorship value. When a company has decided to make in investment in your event as a sponsor, they are committing hard-earned dollars.

The fact that one sponsor invests more financially than another may give one more status and benefits, but all sponsors have something in addition to cash that can be beneficial to both the event and the sponsor. Here are some examples of items that may be available to your sponsors, which they would be willing to provide to your event.

Tangible

- Transportation — company owns a fleet of rental cars or buses
- In-house printing department
- In-house production studio or graphics department
- Giveaway items (left over from another event that your event staff would appreciate) or good to use as door prizes
- The boss' vacation home as a raffle prize
- Preexisting contracts with service providers such as security, waste removal, portable fencing, and restrooms

Intangible

- Membership to a private club — location for social event
- Lives in an exclusive neighborhood next door to a sports figure
- Brother-in-law is a recognized entertainer
- Wife is on a local charity board that can provide event staffing
- Social, recreational, and outside interest connections of the decision-maker or his management team

- Access to mailing lists and databases, or personal business connections who might also be interested in your event

PARTNERSHIP OPPORTUNITIES

Of course, any time you develop a relationship with an entity involved in your event, you want to think of them as a partner in the project. Here, we are using the term *partnership* to distinguish a sponsor with a monetary investment from one with an in-kind donation of products or services in exchange for benefits.

Pros

- The event is provided with product of a higher quality or larger quantity than agreed upon
- Easier access to more product if you run out
- Event staffing
- Community involvement in building relationships with the partner's partners
- Use of their facilities for activities such as sponsor mixers or stuffing giveaway bags
- Use of their staff to stuff the bags
- Media partners may provide more air time and produce the on-air segment

Cons

- The event is provided with product of a lesser quality or smaller quantity than agreed upon
- If you run out of product, there is no ability to restock another product because the partner has purchased the right to have only his brand product served (think colas)
- Disinterested or untrained event staff

- Event staff no-shows
- Relationships with partner's other partners that might not be appropriate for your event
- Media time placement may at times be inappropriate for the event audience
- Orchestrating the transfer of goods and services is far more complicated than depositing a check

IN-KIND VALUE

Valuation of contributed goods and services is another tricky topic. Some partners expect the value of their investment to be equal to the retail price of their product, while some event producers will value the investment at somewhere between 50-80% of the retail value. There is no tried-and-true rule about valuation of in-kind donations. Many agreements are designed to include both cash and product or service.

BEWARE OF UNREQUESTED DONATIONS

It is not unusual for someone involved in the event, usually a committee member or a sponsor, to offer to provide something for free. This situation should be handled with care, as the person truly believes he is doing a service to the event by making the donation; unrequested donors are usually unaware of the new costs incurred by accepting a free offer.

For every line item in your budget there is a production expense involving a product and/or service. If you have budgeted for cupcakes, take a look at what happens when someone insists on accepting donated sheet cakes.

A line item for cupcakes involves:

- Cupcake ordering and delivery
- Cupcake distribution to guests
- Garbage cans to collect cupcake wrappers

A line item for sheet cake involves:

- Sheet cake delivery
- Purchase or rental of plates and forks $$$
- Increased staff to cut the cake $$$
- Cake slice distribution to guests
- More or larger garbage cans to collect plates and utensils $$$
- Increased garbage removal $$$
- Appearance that your event is not "green" in its excess garbage

MORAL: *"free" sheet cakes can be costly*

FUNDRAISERS AND FRIEND-RAISERS

Often when we think of events and sponsorships, we think of nonprofit organizations trying to raise money. This is not always the case. On a previous page under "Sponsorship Benefits," there is a list of the primary, or most obvious, reasons why people or companies wish to become a sponsor. The last bullet point was called, "support a worthy cause."

Using a more generic term, I call it "the feel-good effect." I don't eat Girl Scout cookies, but each year I buy them and donate them to a local hospital. Why? For less than $20, it makes me "feel good."

Life is hard...
sometimes people just want to feel good about something.

In the past decade, it has become fashionably acceptable to get on the bandwagon of specialized causes. If you have a particular interest, no matter how removed it is from the everyday norm, there is most likely an organization that supports it.

You see commercials on late-night TV, celebrities traveling to distant parts of the world, and a request from an organization you have never heard of has most likely graced your mailbox. There are groups for any number of victims of violent crimes, diseases, retired movie animals, armchair travelers, and seniors reentering the workforce. If you can't find the group that's exactly right for you and you have the resources, you can even start your own charity, as we've seen done by the families of cancer survivors.

What these newer groups have in common is that they are not only designed to raise money for their causes, but to raise awareness and build a congregation or community of like-minded people. Unlike individuals' behavior of 50 years ago, when more people were involved in fewer but larger organized groups, today, smaller groups of people are involved in a greater number of groups.

FUNDRAISING EVENTS

Fundraising events are specifically designed to raise monies to be applied to the goods and services provided by the organization.

Information about the organization is threaded through the event.

- Pre-event: invitation, promotional materials, web site

- On-site in the form of speeches, printed programs, dis plays
- Post-event: thank you note, newsletter article, display, or electronic advertising

Common methods of fundraising are:
- Event ticket sales
- Food and beverage sales
- Chance/opportunity tickets, a.k.a. raffle tickets
- Auctions (live and silent)
- Products (books, CDs, cookies, candy)
- Activities (car wash, golf tournaments)
- Sponsorship

Funding is not the only thing attracting sponsors. Sponsoring or hosting "friend-raisers" links the sponsor or host directly to an even more targeted audience than a fundraiser.

"FRIEND-RAISING" EVENTS

Friend-raising events are commonly held to distribute the group's information, bring attention to the cause, and grow the participation in the group.

Why host a friend-raising event?

Friend-raising conjures up images of the good old days as seen in family albums with photos of picnics, bake sales, and barn raisings. Those activities brought special interest groups together in the past just as they can today. Here are some reasons for a get-together:

- Increasing the participation base of the organization serves as a tool to spread the word about the cause of the organization.
- A larger participation base increases the potential giving base.
- Synergy — the like-interest of the group often positions passionate people with little income and lots of time to volunteer next to high-profile people with a big income and little time to volunteer.
- The high-profile people have connections that bring these special interest groups to the media or political forefront.
- Arm-twisting and monetary investments are not the primary focus, and consequently the event may attract an audience that avoids fundraisers.
- Expanding your personal world and business contacts by developing friendships with people who have similar interests.
- Opportunity to join forces with other similar organizations.
- Boosting employee morale by allowing them to be involved in activities they select.
- Low-cost, low-fuss way to spend time with people like yourself.

How to "host" a friend-raising event

Friend-raising events can be as easy as inviting one person to your house for coffee and as complicated as hosting a formal dinner.

Host is the first keyword. *Manageable* is the second keyword. Although rallies in a stadium might be called "friend-raisers," they can lack the sense of intimacy needed to gain the confidence and attention of your targeted audience. Although the people you invite really are a targeted audience, think "personal" when you think of hosting a friend-raiser. Why do I use the word *host?* Because there is time and/or money involved in any interaction.

If you meet someone for coffee and each pays for his own cup, there is no "hosting" money per se, but there is time committed. When the person investing the time and/or money is doing so from a personal basis, without expecting the immediate end result of making money, he or she is acting more as a friend or host than a sponsor.

If 20, 30, or more people are invited to a hosted reception, the same holds true — someone does have to pay the bill and similar benefits are afforded the person paying the bill, but the term "host" is softer, gentler. Yesterday's quilting bees and today's stamping parties are good friend-raising examples.

Locations

- Homes (indoor or outdoor)
- Apartment building or neighborhood clubhouses
- Private clubs (banquet rooms or outdoor facilities)
- Businesses (conference rooms or break rooms)
- Restaurants or coffee shops
- Free public facilities and areas such as libraries and parks
- Paid facilities of mutual interest such as roller rinks, batting cages, bowling alleys, and pool halls
- The gathering rooms of schools, hospitals, and churches

Excuses to get people together

- Introductions (to high-profile people or celebrities)
- Seasonal (back yard garden parties or indoor holiday gatherings)
- Shared experience (hands-on projects, cooking, wine

tasting)
- Mutual interest in a topic (films or books)
- Purpose driven — to accomplish something

The splintering away from mega groups to micro groups allows for a union of people who think with a narrower focus about a particular cause.

The capability of keying words into the Internet search engines makes it possible for anyone looking for a particular group of people with similar interests to be found in mere keystrokes.

Here are some examples of two large organizations that are still going strong, and a few of the newer, more targeted organizations. The information listed below is from their web sites.

American Society for the Prevention of Cruelty to Animals (ASPCA)[2]: regional chapters ASPCA — "The ASPCA was the first humane organization in the Western Hemisphere. Our mission, as stated by our founder, Henry Bergh, in 1866, is 'to provide effective means for the prevention of cruelty to animals throughout the United States.'"

Society for the Prevention of Cruelty to Animals (SPCA)[3] International "founded in 2006 to advance the safety and well-being of animals with programs such as Operation Baghdad Pups Program: a highly successful program helps U.S. troops safely transport home the companion animals they befriend in the war zone.

---

2 American Society for the Prevention of Cruelty to Animals (ASPCA);
  www.aspca.org
3 Society for the Prevention of Cruelty to Animals (SPCA), International;
  www.spcai.org

Operation Baghdad Pups[4] is a logistically challenging program that helps immensely with Post Traumatic Stress Disorder (PTSD). SPCA International receives three to six new requests for help every week from soldiers serving in the Middle East, and their families."

Retrievers & Friends of Southern California, Inc. (RFSC)[5] is "an all-volunteer, non-profit organization devoted to finding homes for Golden Retrievers & Labrador Retrievers, as well as other breeds of dogs as space allows."

Performing Animal Welfare Society (PAWS)[6] founded in 1984 by former Hollywood animal trainer and author Pat Derby and her partner, Ed Stewart. It is "dedicated to the protection of performing animals, to providing sanctuary to abused, abandoned and retired captive wildlife, to enforcing the best standards of care for all captive wildlife, to the preservation of wild species and their habitat and to promoting public education about captive wildlife issues."

American Cancer Society[7] was founded in 1913 as the American Society for the Control of Cancer (ASCC) by 15 prominent physicians and business leaders in New York City. It is "dedicated to helping persons who face cancer. Supports research, patient services, early detection, treatment and education."

---

4 www.spcai.org/baghdad-pups
5 Retrievers & Friends of Southern California, Inc. (RFSC);
   www.retrieversandfriends.com
6 Performing Animal Welfare Society (PAWS); www.pawsweb.org
7 American Cancer Society; www.cancer.org

The National Childhood Cancer Foundation (NCCF)[8] founded in 1989. It is "a nonprofit public benefit charity which raises funds from public and private sources and allocates those revenues to support clinical and biological research conducted at childhood cancer treatment and research centers throughout North America."

Keaton Raphael Memorial for Neuroblastoma, Inc.[9] was founded after Keaton's death in 1998. Says Robyn Raphael, founder and CEO, "In memory of our son we created a nonprofit organization that since inception has remained committed to helping childhood cancer families in Northern California through our Patient Care, Research, Advocacy and Education funds."

DESIGNING THE RIGHT COLLATERAL MATERIALS TO DELIVER THE MESSAGE

Designing the right collateral is required to connect with your audience. Today's software programs enable anyone with time and interest to try their hand at graphics. Some software programs are geared toward beginners and some toward professionals. Bundled software programs usually contain a writing component, numbers component (for spreadsheets), and a graphics component.

Within your organization, volunteers and employees will have different levels of graphics capabilities. There is probably also a professional graphics person on your board or events committee. Whoever this person is, it is important that the designer of the collateral material and the people in the distribution line communicate. Both should understand the profile of the audience, their likes and dislikes, and especially how they receive information.

---

8   The National Childhood Cancer Foundation (NCCF); www.suresearch.org
9   Keaton Raphael Memorial for Neuroblastoma, Inc; www.childcancer.org

Refer back to the pages on identifying your audience — the age group is only the start of understanding who they are and determining the best communication methods to achieve your desired results.

- Here are additional considerations to communicate effectively with your audience:
- Use the proper language to match their level of education.
- Consider regional speech patterns and phrasing.
- Avoid clichés and lingo unless you are absolutely sure they will respond positively.
- Use the shortest sentences and simplest words possible to deliver your message.
- Have several people representing your audience profile review and edit your work for appropriateness.

CAUTION: make sure the person you select to produce your graphics understands both the profile of your target audience and the methods in which the information will be delivered.

MATCHING THE MESSAGE DELIVERY TO THE AUDIENCE (EXAMPLES):

Children:
They don't read, so materials should be directed to their parents, caretakers, grandparents, or other family members.

If people the children interface with speak another language, provide the information in that language.

Teenagers:
Web sites, texting, tweeting, YouTube, cell phones, email, social networking sites, magazines, ezines, graphic novels, comic books

College age:

Web sites, texting, tweeting, YouTube, cell phones, email, social networking sites, magazines, ezines, ebooks, books, graphic novels, comic books

Young adults/new parents/young families:

Web sites, texting, tweeting, YouTube, cell phones, email, social networking sites, flyers, posters, graphic novels, magazines, ezines, ebooks, books

Adults:

Web sites, texting, tweeting, YouTube, cell phones, email, social networking sites, flyers, posters, magazines, ebooks, books

Seniors:

Newspapers, magazines, flyers, posters, direct mail, TV, radio, some usage of web sites, email, ebooks, social networking sites

To communicate effectively with your audience, you'll be using a variety of methods, many of which include print or the written word. These next few pages will serve as a primer and terms you can use as you select the best approach for your audience.

COMMONLY USED COLLATERAL TERMS AND DEFINITIONS

Brochure is a printed piece containing paragraphs of information and images, and is meant to be read. It comes in a variety of formats including:

Single fold — page/s folded in half
Gate fold — outer edges folded to the center
Tri-fold — three folds
Accordion fold — multiple folds

Poster and Flyer is a single piece of paper printed on one or both sides that often includes an image and information presented in short sentences, bullets, and independently placed words. It is meant to attract attention and be read quickly.

Program or Playbill is a document, usually several pages and often stapled, that is distributed on-site at the event and outlines the event schedule/agenda. It lists participants and often is used for paid advertising and sponsor recognition.

Bill stuffer is a promotion piece, usually the same size as the envelope, with enough information to remind or pique the curiosity of the recipient.

Self-mailer is a printed document with proper space allowed on one side to apply an address. The self-mailer requires a means to hold the document closed. It is not intended to require an envelope.

PUBLISHING TERMS AND DEFINITIONS

(Times New Roman and Arial are used in this example)

Typeface or font is the word used to describe the alphabet as it appears graphically on the page.

The word serif refers to little feet-like graphics found at the end of letters. Serif typeface or fonts have a soft, round feeling and are usually used for "body copy," a.k.a. the text or larger, more wordy portion of the document. This paragraph is in Times New Roman, a standard serif font, point size 12.

A basic **sans serif** (without feet, straight angle) typeface is often used for title pages, headlines, and descriptions. This paragraph is in Arial, a standard sans serif font, point size 12.

***NOTE that even though both paragraphs shown above are formatted in the same point size, different fonts require a different amount of space, making the second paragraph, done in the sans serif font called Arial, look larger.

Another font size consideration is the audience who will be reading the document. Rule of thumb is that the older the audience, the larger the font.

DESIGNING THE EVENT
AND THEME

You're probably wondering, and even a bit anxious, about the event and the theme. You're probably thinking, "We're more than halfway through the book and we haven't even touched on what I consider the 'fun' part." That's right. We are more than halfway through the book. It's also right that you may consider designing the event and the theme to be the fun part...which is exactly why that discussion starts here and not on page one.

To the layman or the party planner, the purpose of an event is to be fun. Fun may be an element of the results-driven event, but it is not the focus. The focus is to design an event that produces the results as defined by the client or boss.

Section One discussed applying the concepts of a marketing plan to an event plan. Section Two discussed seeing your event from a results perspective as well as understanding the key management people involved in the event. Section Three looked at the audience and the sponsors. With this foundation laid, now it's time to pull this information together and begin designing the event.

We go through this dissection of the moving parts and people because, generally speaking, identifying with the values of your client and audience offers the highest potential for success. To give an audience an experience they'll enjoy, you first have to understand what they like and how they like it presented.

You think you know your client, sponsors, and audience pretty well by now, but here are a few more considerations:

How do they relate? Most people relate:

    1) Visually

    2) Audit orally

    3) Kinesthetically

What drives their behavior?

- Emotion
- Habit/familiarity
- Having options

The more you know about how your client, sponsors, and audience think and act, the better your chance of producing a successful event.

In designing your event, keep these facts in mind. If your guests will respond well to options, perhaps food stations are a better choice than a plated and served dinner. If they are family-oriented, plan a picnic or afternoon at the zoo. If they attend arts and cultural events, include music and visually stimulating elements in your design.

On the flip side, if your audience is older, consider their ability to hear. Too much sound, too much color, and too much action may be distracting.

Designing a successful event comes from:

➡ Gathering layers of information about your audience

➡ Applying that information to your event elements

➡ Fine-tuning the details to cause the event to appear naturally seamless.

REASONS FOR CORPORATE CELEBRATIONS

High-ranking in the list of corporate excuses for a party are occasions celebrating business success in the form of longevity, excellence, productivity, and change.

Change	New location or name
	New employee
	Assignment
	New hire
	Advancement
Productivity	**Trade recognition**
	LEED certification
	Product launch
Awards	**Industry**
	Employee
	Project
Ongoing	**Client recognition**
	Employee
	Business retention
	New business
Longevity	**Employee service record**
	Association with clients
	Opening of a business branch
	or facility

Types of corporate events

- Groundbreaking
- Grand opening
- Open house
- Product launch
- Recognition dinners
- Employee picnics
- Team building
- Client appreciation
- Awards banquets
- Involvement with charity or nonprofit organization

MILESTONE ANNIVERSARIES

Anniversary-themed events aren't just reserved for weddings. Whether you represent a corporation or nonprofit organization, anniversaries are a great way to celebrate business and reinforce your position in the marketplace.

Terminology often used for milestone anniversaries:

1st Annual	75th Dodranscentennial
5th Quinquennial	100th Centennial
10th Decennial	125th Quasquicentennial
25th Quadranscentennial	150th Sesquicentennial
50th Semicentennial	200th Bicentennial

ANNIVERSARIES (compiled list from various sources)

	Modern (in the U.S.)	Flower	Color
1st	Clocks	Carnation	Yellow
2nd	China	Lily of the Valley	Linen-White
3rd	Crystal, glass	Sunflower	Light Brown
4th	Electrical appliances	Hydrangea	Green
5th	Silverware	Daisy	Turquoise
6th	Wood	Calla Lily	White
7th	Desk set	Freesia	Off-White
8th	Linen, lace	Lilac	Bronze
9th	Leather	Bird of Paradise	Terracotta
10th	Diamond jewelry	Daffodil	Silver
11th	Fashion jewelry	Tulip	Turquoise
12th	Pearls,colored gems	Peony	Oyster-White
13th	Textiles, fur	Chrysanthemum	White
14th	Gold jewelry	Dahlia	Ivory
15th	Watches	Rose	Ruby-Red
20th	Platinum	Aster	Emerald-Green/White
21st	Brass/nickel		Orange
22nd	Copper		Green
23rd	Silver plate		Silver
24th	Musical instruments		Lavender
25th	Silver	Iris	Silver
30th	Diamond	Lily	Green
35th	Jade		Coral
40th	Ruby	Gladiolus	Ruby-Red
45th	Sapphire		Sapphire-Blue
50th	Gold	Yellow roses, violets	Gold
75th	Diamond		Diamond
100th	Centennial: Often representative image and color of the celebrant		

PUTTING THE PIECES TOGETHER

Where do you start designing the event? You already have. All those hours of research are now going to line up like ducks in a row. You know the likes, dislikes, and habits of your audience. You know the expectation of the client, sponsors, and partners. And, you have some information on the vendors that will be required.

The word *design* is often associated with events, but in the "business" of events, it takes on a different character. There are many great artists who have come to the event industry and become very successful event designers.

Richard Carbotti, owner of Perfect Surroundings, Inc. in Rhode Island, is a graduate of the Parsons School of Design in Manhattan and the Newhouse School of Public Communications at Syracuse University.

Unlike an artist with a brush, an event designer is more like an assemblage artist who pulls together bits and pieces into a grand mosaic.

In the industry of event production, these bits and pieces are often represented by specialized vendors, including:

Audio/Visual	Staging
Lighting	Tenting
Catering	Floral
Props and décor	Furnishings, rentals
Graphics	Writing
Set designers	Script writers
Public relations	Media relations
Marketing	Collateral materials
Lodging	Venues
Drayage	Warehouse

Administrative services	Unions
Event staffing	Casual labor
Photography	Videography
Entertainment	Activities
Talent, speakers	Dignitaries
Restrooms	Special effects
Transportation	Valet parking
Awards and trophies	Premiums, giveaways

The list goes on and on as it gets more specialized.

WORKING GLOBALLY OR OUTSIDE OF YOUR HOME BASE

Depending on the scope of the event, its location, budget, and purpose, professionals are brought together locally, regionally, and even internationally. It is not unusual with a high-budget, high-profile event to have the design and production team consisting of the best professionals in their field from around the world. With Internet communications access, it has become commonplace to work on projects anytime, anyplace.

Just as in movie credits that list workers from the location where the film was shot, event producers also hire locals. Locals are hired for the obvious reasons that they know the lay of the land, the jurisdictions, and the nuances, and they have the contacts to make things happen.

Many international companies have offices throughout the world. National conglomerates, such as tenting and furnishings, have retail showrooms and warehouses in many states. The benefit of using a national company is that your business with them is already established and the planner can make an easy transition from one storefront to another because he is familiar with their style of doing business.

Some of the larger companies also stock different items best suited for their particular regions. Tiki huts and grass skirting may be warehoused by a showroom based in the tropical climate, whereas wine barrel bars and rustic furniture can be found in the wine growing part of the country. And remember prop houses — areas with filming and theater will have resources for props galore to spice up your theme.

CONSIDERATIONS WHEN WORKING ON INTERNATIONAL PROJECTS OR OUTSIDE OF YOUR HOME BASE

- Time differences
- Date line
- Language
- Customs (societal)
- Customs (border crossings)
- Currency exchange
- Signals (such as cell phone use)
- Transportation
- Food and beverage service
- Accommodations
- Regulations, permits, insurance
- Power (electrical)
- General expectations

WORKING WITH PROFESSIONALS

Every town has event professionals trained in their specialty. Many have trade school education, while others have hands-on experience. All are an asset to your event.

Review the vendor list and you'll see some of the pros you'll be working with. Whether this is your first event or you have done hundreds, working with professionals makes your job easier because they know what they're doing, and can help you through problem areas in your plan. They have connections with others in the industry, and can save you time and money getting the job done right.

Investing, both monetarily and with time, in "scouting" the area in which you'll be working will eliminate surprises.

Location-scouting tips

- Proximity of lodging to the event site
- Availability of local public transportation
- Big box or warehouse- type stores — food, supplies
- Local suppliers — tents, furnishings
- Location of hospitals, police, fire
- Access road to venue
- Airports and trains
- Availability of professional, event staffing, and laborers

International Special Events Society

On the topic of professionals and who they associate with, this is a good place to give a plug for the International Special Events Society (ISES).

ISES is the professional association of those involved in the special events industry. As with any professional organization, members are bonded with a like interest in the industry and are able to easily communicate because they speak the same event language, share the same ethics and values, and have similar education and training. ISES offers members easy access and relationships to other members around the world. For this reason, there is a high rate of success with ISES members working as a team on events in the United State or abroad. ISES has chapters located all over the planet.

Certified Special Event Professional (CSEP) is the hallmark of professional achievement in the special events industry. As of this writing, the designation of CSEP belongs to less than 300 professionals worldwide.

www.ISES.org
Headquarters:
401 N. Michigan Ave Chicago, IL 60611-4267 USA
312-321-6853 or 800-688-4737 Fax: 312-673-6953

OTHER ORGANIZATIONS RELATED TO THE EVENT INDUSTRY

International:
- International Special Events Society (ISES)
- Meeting Planners International (MPI)
- International Festival & Events Association (IFEA)

National:
- American Marketing Association (AMA)
- Public Relations Society of America (PRSA)
- National Association of Catering Executives (NACE)

Statewide (examples in California):
- California Society of Association Executives (CSAE)
- CalFest (California and Nevada Festivals & Events Association)

Local (examples in the Sacramento area):
- American Marketing Association, Sacramento Valley Chapter (AMASV)
- Sacramento Public Relations Association (SPRA)

Unions (examples of those with local chapters):
- Stagehands
- Electricians
- Plumbers
- Contractors

DECIDING ON THE STYLE OF EVENT

If you're not already working on a real event, refer to the page called "Any Excuse for a Party" in Section One, and pick a topic around which you can develop an imaginary event.

The profiles of your client, sponsors, partners, and audience will have led you to a decision on the style of event you will present. After identifying the purpose and the specific objectives, it's time to consider how you will make them come to life through the event. Remember to give your event legs you should be thinking about applying these techniques before, during, and after the event.

DELIVERING THE CORPORATE MESSAGE

- Signage, banners
- Speeches from the stage
- Behind-the-scenes prerecorded or live announcements
- Flyers, posters
- Programs, playbills
- Giveaway items — books, CDs, DVDs, flash drives, workbooks

SPONSOR INVOLVEMENT

- On-site presence (booth, signage, event staff, give aways, announcements)
- Celebrity appearance (representing the sponsor)
- Stage emcee
- Product display or sampling
- Showcase — live stage presentation

SPONSOR RECOGNITION

- Visibility on event and client web site, link to the sponsor's web site

- Newsletter articles, big check photo
- Promotion and publicity
- Use of sponsor's facilities
- Inclusion of sponsor's staff

An event is a marketing tool; it is the vehicle used to deliver the objectives.

THE HIERARCHY OF DECISION MAKING

Consider how the goals and objectives you identified lend themselves to the overall style and structure of the event. The numbers of elements and details in a seemingly simple event can take pages of single-spaced line items. Where to start is often a stumbling block because each decision you make positively or negatively impacts decisions further down the line. If the client has indicated a "must-have" element, such as a particular talent act, food, or venue, that should be at the top of your decision-making list. After that, think in terms of size, as in the size of the decision.

Visualize your event plan as an inverted ice cream cone. The biggest decisions are the base and as the decisions get smaller they rise to the top. In the end, these tiny decisions can add that extra little touch to the event or they can be left unattended without impacting the outcome of the event.

FIRST — MAKE THE REALLY BIG DECISIONS

- Primary purpose (goals and objectives)
- Business, social, both
- Fundraiser or friend-raiser
- Estimated number of guests

FINANCIAL

- Budget estimate
- Hosted or not hosted
- Fundraising goal
- Ticket sales or by invitation
- Other income (raffles, auctions, product sales)
- Staffing/production
- Permits, security, insurance, safety

STYLE

- Formal or informal
- Morning, afternoon, evening
- Attire (black-tie, business, resort casual)
- Décor (rented, created, borrowed, available on-site)
- On-site or off-site
- Parking and transportation
- Setup and strike time

VENUE

- On-site or off-site
- Parking and transportation
- Setup and strike time
- Permits, security, insurance, safety

SITE PLAN

- Main stage
- Breakout rooms
- Event headquarters
- Pre-function area
- Green room

FOOD AND BEVERAGE

- Food
    Sit-down
    Buffet
    Stations

FOOD SERVICE

- Passed
    Plated
    Family style
    White glove

BEVERAGE CONSUMPTION

- Hosted
    No-host
    Tickets and distribution

BEVERAGE TYPE

- Alcoholic or nonalcoholic or both

ALCOHOL

- Beer and wine
- Hard liquor
- Hard liquor
- House
- Call
- Top shelf

PRESENTATION OR PERFORMANCES

- Talent
- Special protocol requirements for high-profile partici pants
- Entertainment
- Activities
- Awards
- Speeches
- Projections

TECHNICAL

- Staging
- Lighting
- Audio/visual
- Unions

COLLATERAL — GRAPHICS BEFORE THE EVENT

- Invitation, brochure, RSVP
- Display ad
- Poster, flyer, bill stuffer

COLLATERAL — GRAPHICS AT THE EVENT

- Directional signage
- Informational signage
- Banners (logo)
- Site maps
- Programs and playbills
- Schedules
- Name badges
- Table signs
- Giveaways and swag bags

COLLATERAL — GRAPHICS AFTER THE EVENT

- Thank you notes
- Display ads
- Web site
- Personalized photo recognition

PROPS AND DÉCOR

- Décor
    Rented
    Created
    Borrowed
    Available on-site
- Floral
    Cut
    Live
    Silk
    Applied (like a parade float)
- Special effects
    Light shows
    Fireworks
    Cirque-style performers

BASIC RENTALS

- Furnishings
- Tables
- Chairs
- Linens
- Tabletop (china, crystal, utensils)

MISCELLANEOUS RENTALS

- Champagne fountains
- Aisle runners
- Outdoor heaters and lighting
- Lecterns and podiums
- Fencing
- Stanchions and red carpet
- Portable bars
- Food service hot and cold equipment such as chafing dishes, refrigerators, etc.
- Chuppah (bride and groom canopy in a Jewish wedding)
- Regional specialty items such as Tiki huts and wine barrel bars
- Theatrical props

SELECTING THE THEME

Themes are as plentiful as drops of water in the ocean. Often the most successful themes are easy to recognize and understand. In addition to naming the theme, the manner in which it takes form is also an open playing field. If there is a single element to an event that separates one designer from another, it is how he or she envisions the theme and adds a personal touch to make it special.

When first considering a theme, understand the obvious implications of the theme, then extrapolate from there. The décor is the face of the event, the site dressed in party clothes. Consider what it will look like, keeping in mind the formality of the event, audience profile, ticket price, and so on.

There are two approaches to designing the on-site visual: either design the invitation and then select pieces of décor that replicate the invitation graphics, or start with your vision of the event site and apply similar images to the invitation.

I like to use a combination of the two. First, imagine or sketch the big picture that guests will see when they arrive. Something in this imagined or real picture is sure to attract your attention as a possible stand-alone image or idea for the graphics used in the invitation, poster, program, and other collateral pieces.

Next, sketch an invitation or poster. It will probably contain a new graphic element that can be adapted back to the décor. Working in this manner creates a visual continuum between the three-dimensional event and the two-dimensional pre- and post-promotion and publicity.

Whereas the reason for the event may be to celebrate an anniversary, the theme could denote the number of anniversaries — such as a 25th or 50th anniversary using gold or silver, or the corresponding flower, as its theme — or it could relate directly to those celebrating the anniversary by taking on a military, dog-lover, or hippie theme.

It's easier and more successful to design the invitations and other graphics to introduce the event theme and site you've already selected, than to design the invitations first, then try to match the décor to your invitations.

THEME IDEAS

Any of the ideas listed can be used as a springboard to a great new idea

SPECIAL INTEREST:	Colors	Automobiles
	Books	Cooking
	Clothing	Gardening
	Stock market	Real estate
	Movies	Photograph
	Scrapbooking	Travel
SPECIAL EVENTS:	Olympics	Royal wedding
	Eclipse	Inauguration
	Shuttle launch	Premiere
SPORTS (outdoor):	Skiing	Kite flying
	Skateboarding	Roller skating
	Football	Baseball
	Bicycling	Ice skating
	Golf	Auto racing
	Swimming	Tennis
	Boating	Geocaching
SPORTS (indoor):	Ping-Pong	Darts
	Shuffleboard	Card games
	Air hockey	Arcade games
PACKAGED THEMES:	Casino	Beach party
	Rock 'n' roll	Superhero
	Drive-in	Western

HOLIDAYS:	President's Day	St. Patrick's Day
	Memorial Day	Fourth of July
	Columbus Day	Thanksgiving
	Veteran's Day	Labor Day
	New Year's	

INTERNATIONAL:	Cinco de Mayo	Mardis Gras
	Bastille Day	Kite Day
	May Day	Dia de los Muertos

RELIGIOUS:	Holidays	Celebrations
	Rites of passage	

SEASONS:	Winter	Spring
	Summer	Fall
	Solstice	Leap year

SPECIAL DAYS:	Groundhog Day	April Fools' Day
	Sadie Hawkins	Blue Moon
	Friday the 13th	Leap year

BLACK AND WHITE THEME DÉCOR (EXAMPLE):

Building the idea from the obvious to the interesting

Tabletop option 1
   Solid color black linens and napkins
   White china, stemmed crystal

Tabletop option 2
   Alternating solid color black linens and napkins
   White china with black rim, stemmed crystal

Tabletop option 3
>Textured solid color black linens and napkins
>Shaped white china and black china, glass tumblers

Tabletop option 4
>Floral print black and white table linens and solid
>>textured napkins
>White shaped china and black glass goblets

---

*At a formal dinner, use black napkins to avoid covering the tuxedos
and black dresses with lint from white napkins.*

THE DESIGNER'S SIGNATURE

In Section Two we discussed the "director's signature." Because of the complexity of events, it is easy for the director to get spread thin in addressing all the details. "If only I had just one thing to focus on instead of a thousand," or "Why is this responsibility on my plate?" The answer to the second question is because you're in charge. The answer to the first is that you haven't yet identified that one special thing that will sustain your interest. You haven't identified your "signature" piece of the event. It is your secret desire to get your signature piece right that will motivate you through other, less glamorous phases of the production process.

Because of the strong connection between the director and the event, it is not unusual that the director's signature is also the event's signature.

In discussing the design of the event, the same holds true. If someone on your committee serves as the designer, he has been selected because of his expertise — allow him that small opportunity to surprise you with an element that will cause the attendees to remember the table or décor in the event venue.

Caveat to all signature elements:

    It fits within the budget

    The idea enhances the purpose and theme of the event

    Implementation does not require excess amounts of time

If you are both the director and the designer, it's time to change hats and add that special touch to the décor and/or tabletop. There can be multiple signatures (director, designer, caterer, graphics, tabletop) within an event as long as the signatures all work harmoniously to create an overall special effect and provide a great memory for the attendees.

Signatures allow people in charge of different elements of the event to identify the one special thing that will personally bond them to the event.

NOTE: rental companies have showrooms where you can mix and match tabletop basic and accessories to create your own unique design.

Here are some examples of simple effective ideas for signatures and simple giveaways that I have used in events:

- Mascot Conga Line
- A "wall hammering" to kick off a building remodel
- New-Orleans-style funeral for the rededication of a cemetery
- Bookmarks as flyers for an author presentation
- Twin stilt-walkers on the state capitol grounds to force the media to take long shots and include the capitol dome in the background

- Exploding confetti-filled faux champagne bottles representing a toast to the grand opening of a building
- Catering staff in hard hats and safety vests serving appetizers from industrial dust pans (new and unused) at a high-rise topping-off party
- Using branded wooden shipping containers to create walls and divide the space inside a warehouse venue
- Tented restroom and lobby areas posing as art galleries
- Signature drinks, look-alikes, costumed ethnic entertainers
- from the one normally used at the venue or by the caterer
- Change the entrance from the front door to the side door
- Mardi Gras beads, boas, masks, costumes, washable tattoos, hats, prizes, photos, and always a take-home gift for the guests

PICKING THE RIGHT VENUE FOR YOUR EVENT

Whether you're holding an event at your business headquarters, one of your facilities in a different town or county, or at a private club, conference center, or hotel, all venues have some of the same attributes, both pros and cons.

Each venue will present challenges particular to that facility. Some will have challenges in every aspect of your event, from the contract negotiations through the strike. Some will present so few challenges, you'll wonder if you forgot to ask critical questions.

Event sites and event elements will always raise issues of insurance, permits, and security. Food and beverage, entertainment, activities, parking, and ease of access for guests and vendors are also high on the consideration list.

Here we're addressing capabilities and downfalls of venues. The best advice I can give is, "Don't fall in love with the venue." Think of selecting the venue in the same manner you would select your car. If the car isn't large enough and rugged enough to haul your family and dogs on a ski trip, you wouldn't select it. Pass on the venue that doesn't provide the atmosphere and attributes matching your event. It's easier, and usually less expensive, to keep looking till you find a venue that matches your event profile than to reengineer a venue that doesn't.

Generally speaking, your event will either be held on-site or off-site. Here are basic definitions of those terms.

On-site means that much of what you will need to produce the event is available at or through the venue.

Off-site means either that everything you need must be taken to a temporary installation, or that you are moving your guests to a venue other than the primary venue.

Six general categories of venues:

    1) Hotel and conference center
    2) Convention center
    3) Private club
    4) Private home
    5) Business facility
    6) Temporary installation

"Where's the bathroom?" is asked by the majority of guests at any event and by vendors and event staff during setup. Make sure the locations of bathrooms are clearly marked.
"Tips on Avoiding Surprises: What to Ask Before Renting a Venue" is located at the end of this chapter.

SITE INSPECTIONS

Hotel photos rarely show difficult entrances, such as flights of stairs or steep driveways. Because the entrance and ease of access is the first thing your guests will experience, all properties should be visited before selecting one as the site for your event.

Younger guests will enjoy stark surroundings and loud music, but older guests will expect comfy chairs and signage with letters large enough to read from a distance. Until you experience the facility through the eyes of your guest, you will not know if it is acceptable.

Often, unannounced site inspections reveal information not shown to you on formal guided tours. Between 11 a.m. and 2 p.m. is a good time to walk the halls of a hotel and peek in the bedrooms or ask for an informal tour. If you are booking standard rooms with your event, ask to see the standard rooms and the suites, in case you have a guest speaker or official who requires a larger room with more amenities.

When blocking rooms, a suite is often included in the room block and is used for special hospitality occasions. If this room is also used as a sleeping room, be mindful of who is assigned to the room. You don't want to have someone who shoos VIP guests out too early, nor do you want someone who tempts guests to party late into the night. Noon is also a good time to inspect a banquet room while it's filled with guests. This allows you to see how close the tables are set together and how the wait staff sets the tables. If a business meeting is taking place, a registration area will more likely be found in the pre-function area in the morning, and break/coffee service will often be found in the pre-function area in the afternoon.

HOTELS AND CONFERENCE CENTERS:

The bonus with hotels and conference centers is that they have sleeping rooms and you can keep your guests under one roof. They usually have restaurants, bars with entertainment, swimming pools, a gym or exercise room, a gift shop, a business center, and many have spas — great for spouses and after meetings. They can offer suggestions for local vendors such as florists, bakers, and talent.

Hotels and conference centers come in all shapes and sizes, from the low-end cost with few amenities to high-end luxury hotels with landing pads. In between are independently owned mid-price hotels and chain hotels.

While you may receive more personalized service at an independent hotel, if your event is annual and takes place in different cities, you may get a better rate with a multi-year agreement at a hotel chain.

And don't forget the family-owned bed and breakfast, cabin clusters by the sea, a vacation rental with a view of Central Park, or a even cruise ship. If you're thinking about a "road trip" theme, taking over a roadside motel will give your event built-in atmosphere.

The downside to hotels is that you must use their food and beverage department, and usually their audio/visual department. It is not unusual for these services to be high-priced, have a limited selection, and have a low value for the cost.

You can't teach the kitchen staff how to serve hot food and create a recipe for interesting chicken, and you can't ensure that the equipment will run unless you pay extra to have a hotel A/V technician for every break-out room. But you can negotiate for free sleeping rooms, to have room charges waived, or for free Internet access.

CONVENTION CENTERS:

Convention centers were designed for flexibility of use and large gatherings. Wide-open spaces and moveable air walls allow the space to be reconfigured to meet the needs of a large group. They have private loading zones and a lot of roll-up doors, ramps, and service elevators, which make access easy for vendors — unless they're under construction. There's electricity everywhere and plenty of restrooms.

The facilities are usually laden with cement and are cold, both in temperature and ambiance. Although staging and A/V companies will be satisfied with the ease of using scissor lifts and transporting their equipment inside the barren space, it can be a challenge for prop and décor people to fill the halls with enough fluff to create an intimate atmosphere unless they have a hefty budget.

For most convention centers, the wait staff is capable of serving many people in the shortest amount of time and the operations staff works like a well-oiled machine. For the best experience at a convention center, you need to train your event staff to think in terms of the big-scale experience and to focus on efficiency. Put on your game face — super-huge venues can test your will and personality.

PRIVATE CLUBS:

Private clubs offer a sense of being special from the outset. They also come with rules. Clubs are used for entertaining, so they have a variety of room sizes and are usually decorated to match the season. You can use one or many of the rooms. The staff is almost always impeccable, and the food is usually very good both in taste and presentation. The upside is that private clubs have high standards on a daily basis, and these standards transfer over to special events.

The downside is the same: the high daily standards transfers exactly to the special event. The same great food on the same great plate, the same napkin fold, the same wait staff uniform. The same stage, the same centerpieces, the same décor. For those who are unfamiliar with the venue, this is a treat. For those familiar with the location, the event can feel ho-hum if you don't add your own special flair.

To that end, before booking a private club, find out what is allowed, in addition to their normal way of doing business, and if you can bring in outside vendors.

Also, remember to ask about other events taking place at the venue; the drumbeat from the live band at the wedding reception, or sugar-loaded teenagers at a Bar/Bat Mitzvah celebration might not provide the proper background sound for your installation dinner.

To change the everyday look of a table setup, ask the banquet captain to show you the napkin fold options and select one that best represents your theme and is not used at the club on a daily basis.

CONSIDERATIONS WHEN USING UNUSUAL VENUES AND TEMPORARY INSTALLATIONS (HOMES, BUSINESSES, WAREHOUSES, STREETS, PARKS, PARKING LOTS, ETC.)

Facilities in the business of entertaining and dining already have the proper permits, licenses, insurance, and security in place.

Before committing to use a venue that does not normally provide food and beverage service or is not normally used as an event site, research the facility requirements to determine what you must provide to produce the event you envision on the property. You may find the cost of accommodating these requirements exceeds the value of using the site. No rental fee is a bad reason to plan an event at a site because "free" is followed by the expenses required to bring an unusual venue up to event standards.

Think about these necessities.

Permits	HVAC
Licenses	Staging
Insurance	Lighting
Vendor and guest access	Audio/visual
Security	Furnishings
Restrooms	Tabletop
Parking	Props and décor
Temporary kitchens	Communications

Private homes and unusual venues may already have contracts in place for needed event services such as security, waste removal, and restrooms.

PRIVATE HOMES

Private homes have an innate ambiance of warmth and reflect the interests of the homeowners. Some homes are designed for entertaining with wide-open spaces, great rooms, media rooms, built-in, outdoor kitchens and living spaces, and lots of space for parking and access for vendors.

Today's engineering technology allows the pool to be covered and turned into a dance floor, or for the installation of a clear-top tent for star gazing.

People who like to entertain usually have homes designed for entertaining. Homes with lots of knickknacks filling their rooms from floor to ceiling are not likely to be the best choice for an event venue.

In addition to the physical layout of the home, the personality of the homeowner plays a big role in the success of the event. A homeowner may be a gracious host or hostess for a manageable dinner party for six or eight, but can become overwhelmed after agreeing to a company party or a wedding for more than 50.

When planning an event at a private home, make sure the homeowner has had similar experience with events of the size and detail you're suggesting. Testing a private home on your event can result in electrical failure, parking issues, clogged toilets and garbage disposals, oven fires, broken treasures, and any one of a list of home issues that only occur when the house is overloaded with guests.

PLACE OF BUSINESS

Benefits of holding an event at your place of business:

1) If it's an employee event, they're already on-site and you eliminate transportation issues.

2) If you're inviting guests to an after-hours event, you already have the parking and some of the crowd/event accommodation needs already in place (restrooms, electricity, and water).

3) You already know the capabilities of the facility and what you'll need to bring in.

4) You may already have contracts with needed vendors such as security.

The major downside of using your business facility is that you have to transform it to make it a very special place and the transformation can be disruptive to normal business. Think about the areas you might be able to use: waiting room, conference rooms, warehouse, parking lots, and cafeteria.

Many businesses take advantage of using on-site outdoor areas or warehouse space and transforming them through temporary tenting, props, décor, audio/visual, lighting, and staging.

As with convention centers, warehouses are huge and sterile when empty. Large décor budgets are needed to transform a warehouse into a warm, friendly environment.

You can effectively, and inexpensively, reduce the size of your warehouse or outdoor open area by repositioning trucks or pallets of product to encircle a manageable event space. Save money and make the space more intriguing by including the warehouse equipment and clients' product into the décor design.

Reset the auto shutoff of the lights and air conditioning, and reset the sprinkler to auto-on, if the event is to be held outside.

UNEXPECTED VENUES

People often remember a venue more than the event. Keep your eye open for an unfinished or empty building, vacant land, and large parking lots — including parking structures. If you have the budget and can acquire the permits and insurance, any raw space can be turned into a cool event venue.

UNDER A FREEWAY — *BURBANK'S NEW YEAR'S EVE PARTY 2011*

Kicking off of their centennial anniversary, *100 Ways to Celebrate,* the City of Burbank held a New Year's Eve party on a dead-end street under the busy Interstate 5 freeway. The site was in an industrial section of town, a block from the warehouse, a.k.a. float barn, where community volunteers built a float titled "Centennial Celebration" for the 2011 Tournament of Roses parade.

Installed in the venue were a stage, a projection screen, illuminated tables, lighting, heaters, and furnishings. Columns supporting the freeway were wrapped with fabric and up-lit to serve as the backdrop to buffet tables filled with hot and cold foods, desserts, coffee, juice, and hot chocolate with marshmallows. Education and information booths, as well as activities, were scattered throughout the venue. A live band, face painting, coloring tables, stilt walkers, and a close-up magician entertained the crowd.

Guests toured the float barn, talked to the volunteers and designers, and purchased bunches of unused flowers. The float was repositioned onto the street where a crowd gathered to hear speeches, watch the animation test, and see the float drive off to the parade staging area. The event was over by 9 p.m. No business was interrupted, and the police were already on-site to escort the float.

The event attracted a family crowd that swelled to about 5,000 community well-wishers excited to see their self-built float take off for its review New Year's Day in the Pasadena Tournament of Roses Day Parade. The Burbank entry won the 2011 Founders Trophy for the most beautiful entry built and decorated by volunteers.

IN A CEMETERY — *GOLD RUSH CEMETERY REDEDICATION*

Established in 1874, the Matthew Kilgore Cemetery is one of the earliest pioneer cemeteries in the Sacramento region. The cemetery land had been sold as part of a bankruptcy proceeding in the 1950s, and years of neglect and ghoulish vandalism had made it a forgotten piece of the California Gold Rush history.

After a two-year, $1 million restoration project, it was time for celebration. One goal was to increase community awareness, so the event was designed to provide the media with plenty of interesting stories and great visuals.

On May 18, 2007, the pioneer era cemetery was re-dedicated "New Orleans style." At precisely 11 a.m., two, white Percheron horses, donned in official horse mourning attire, pulled an undertaker carriage carrying a casket of flowers representing the souls of the dead.

The procession included city dignitaries twirling parasols, three clergy, a cart with two recovered headstones, and jubilant participants waving commemorative white hankies and dancing to the Hallelujah Brass Band as they passed through the gates of Matthew Kilgore Cemetery.

Historic displays, an emotionally charged ceremony, Dixieland music, and a down-home barbecue rounded out the celebration attended by almost 400.

IN A WAREHOUSE — *FRUIT-PACKING COMPANY CELEBRATES 100 YEARS*

In July 2005, 300 friends, associates, and relatives of Paul A. Mariani celebrated his legacy at the 100th anniversary of Mariani Fruit Packing Co., Inc. in Vacaville, CA. Four generations of Marianis, aged three months old to 85 years old, reunited for the first all-family photo in 50 years.

The company's 50,000-square-foot warehouse was reconfigured into a reception and dining area by creating 12-foot walls from wooden fruit crates bearing the company's name. The event featured ten decades of historical still life displays, a 1950s pickup truck filled with dried fruit, a video presentation, dinner with Mariani fruit-inspired recipes, and hand-painted memento ornaments.

The company's new logo was installed on the building just prior to the event and showcased on wait staff aprons, cocktail napkins, and on thank you cards and gift bags of dried fruit.

More than 200 live, 12-foot to 20-foot fruit trees, up-lit with flashlights, transformed the dining area into an orchard.

The event was over by 10 p.m., and the facility returned to its former working state within five hours. When employees arrived for work the next morning, there was no indication that the warehouse had been transformed into a venue for a milestone event held the night before.

IN A PARKING LOT — *CITY CELEBRATES FIVE YEARS*

Ten weeks of planning led to the 5th anniversary celebration for the city of Rancho Cordova. In a community outreach effort, city council members hosted a series of five neighborhood barbecues scheduled on the five weeks preceding the official City Hall ceremony.

All events were branded with an anniversary image, which was also used on print, broadcast, and electronic collateral throughout the year and throughout the city.

Production of the main event came in 20% under budget, while the attendance of more than 2,000 guests exceeded the original guest estimate of 500 to 750 by 266%.

On a summer night in the City Hall parking lot, more than 2,000 city residents of diverse nationalities spanning four generations attended the city of Rancho Cordova's 5th anniversary. The aroma of barbecued hamburgers lured guests in one direction, while an 18-piece dance band with costumed professional dancers got the crowd moving on the dance floor under the faux band shell. A marching band, cheerleaders, 12-piece banjo band, face painters, balloon artists, community booths, and thousands of branded, take-home goodies delighted the crowd. The ceremonial finale was a confetti "toast" shot by council members from papier-mâché champagne bottles.

SIDE-BY-SIDE OUTDOOR EVENTS LOOK OF ONE BIG FESTIVAL

The First 5 Sacramento Children's' Celebration is perceived as one festival, but is actually two independent events taking place simultaneously. We have two of almost everything: contracts, insurance, permits, security, medical, talent, and event staff.

Perhaps the most unique element of the Children's Celebration is the Mascot Conga Line, originally conceived to move a group of people from the main entertainment stage (inside gated Fairytale Town) to the resource expo in the park. Much like cotton candy at the fair, or popcorn at the movies, the Mascot Conga Line has become the signature activity of the Children's Celebration. Children and adults alike hop in line to touch the back of someone touching the back of someone touching the back of their favorite mascot. It's simply amazing...a no-cost idea worth millions in smiles.

Here's a snapshot of what 7,068 attendees experienced in six hours at the 8th Annual in 2010: 68 educational booths; 40,634 give-away items; 20 dentists and hygienists performing 1,053 dental screenings; 50 hearing tests; 110 vaccines and immunizations; 11 live performances by costumed, ethnic entertainers; 938 kids fingerprinted by 10 Sheriff's Explorers; two fire trucks and one ambulance; mounted patrolmen; 1,250 book bags with books in English and Spanish; 400 washable tattoos; a 30-foot coloring mural; one skinned knee; a block-long Mascot Conga Line...and a swell time had by all!

TEMPORARY INSTALLATIONS

Using a combination of carpenters, electricians, and tents, temporary installations have the potential to be more spectacular simply because the venue is specifically designed to accommodate the needs of the particular event. Designers with a flair for architecture shine in this arena.

Tent height, subfloor, and staging offer the opportunity for different levels inside or outside the tents. The structure itself offers a clear visual destination for your guests and lets them know they are special. Clear "skins" allow you to have a clear view of the sky or garden, while using solid skins enables you to project on the roof or walls. Functional French doors, stairs, shaped windows, tent liners, swagging, and your choice of carpet make temporary build-to-suit venues a perfect choice for special occasions.

Because of the cost and installation/tear-down time involved in temporary installations, a wise idea is to use them for more than one event. If you're planning a groundbreaking, precede that with a private reception, and then a public open house after the main event. Staging fundraisers, either before or after, is always a good use of a special space.

When presenting several events in the same venue you are able to reuse rentals already on-site. Staging a pre-event at the same time of day as the real event provides the opportunity to test the facility and make any necessary changes before the real event. Slight variation in the lighting, table configuration, and linens can drastically change the look to a new theme without the initial major expense.

Specialty tents, including geodesic domes and Indian-style tents with abundant luxury draping, have become popular both as stand-alone venues and as additions to a major installation. Specialty tents are often used for registration, VIP receptions, and to attract attention to a certain part of the larger venue. You'll also see specialty tents at trade shows and traditional venues such as hotels and convention centers, where they are used to attract attention or for similar special gathering areas.

TENT RENTALS

Temporary installations offer the client the opportunity to design the space to specifically fit the requirements of the event. A tent can be as simple as four walls and a canopy, or as complicated as in needed to enclose an entire city of activities.

For a client with ample open, outdoor space available at his place of business, it is often preferred to bring the event to the people rather than to transport the people to the event. Tents are used in groundbreakings, sporting events, conventions, emergency and disaster situations, and in any one of a thousand situations where shelter needs to be provided.

With the proper installation, permitting, insurance, and safety, tents can house kitchens, bathrooms, fleets of vehicles, and can serve as living or working space. Tented temporary venues can have floors, doors, windows, lighting, and HVAC.

Because of their flexibility in size, shape, and capabilities, tents are preferred by many planners who practice designing events from the ground up, and who are not reliant on using the four walls of a preexisting structure.

TENTING TERMS: KNOW THE LINGO[10]

Tent: Temporary structure usually supported by poles or a frame and covered with flexible walls such as vinyl, canvas, or fabric.

Skin/Panels: Vinyl fabric, usually solid or clear, used for the canopy, walls, and windows.

Cathedral windows: Shaped, clear vinyl inserted into a tent wall to serve as a window.

Canopy: Frame with top only (no side walls).

Pop-up tent: Measures between 10-by-10 feet and 16-by-16 feet. Folds up to fit in the back seat of your car. Often used for backyard parties. Event planners usually have several on site to cover unexpected situations or to use as a quick shade tent. Can be staked into the ground but often are not. A "do-it-yourself" tent, easy for a novice to "pop" open and erect.

---

[10] Sidebar from feature article "Gotcha Covered" by Ingrid E. Lundquist, CSEP; Northern California Meetings + Events magazine, Spring 2010

Frame tent: Poles fit together to make a frame covered by skins. The canopy stretches over the rafter poles to form a pitched shape. Width ranges from 5 to 50 feet; length unlimited; 8- to 12-foot wall height; crown height proportionate to the width of the tent.

Festival or Pagoda tent: Frame tent with a high peak, allowing the canopy skin to sculpt down in a soft curve to the corners of the frame. Often a flag or pennant is secured to the peak of the canopy, creating a "festive" look. Referred to as a pagoda tent because of its pagoda-like shape.

Marquee tent: A long, narrow, tunnel-like tent, with or without sidewalls, that serves as a pedestrian entrance to the event venue.

Teepee: Three poles lashed together like a tripod and covered with skin.

Porte-cochére: An entrance canopy for cars to be driven under (allowing guests to be dropped off under shelter in inclement weather), often connected to a marquee tent and/or a red carpet.

Bale-ring tents: Think big-top circus. This tent has a main pole, or multiple center poles. The skin is attached to the bale ring around the center pole or poles. Hoisting the ring up by pulleys (via elephant- or people-power) raises the "big top." Quarter poles and perimeter poles are installed to adequately distribute the weight of the big top.

Push-pole tents: Similar to a bale-ring tent, except the poles are manually pushed into place. Width: 20 to 120 feet.

Guy lines: Ropes or ratchet straps used to stabilize the tent frame to the ground.

Stakes: Long metal objects with one dull-pointed end and a bulb end. They are hammered into the ground and guy lines are attached to stabilize the tent. Staking is used in dirt areas, and on asphalt. Standard industry stakes are 42 inches; shorter stakes are used for smaller tents.

Water barrels: Fifty-five-gallon barrels filled with water and tied to tent poles. Used to stabilize tents when staking is not permitted. Very large tents may require cement blocks or water ballast weighing thousands of pounds.

Clear span: The inside of a tent with no pole obstruction. Also refers to a structure created from a series of arches using *keder* technology, which involves channels built into frame rails. Frame rails, straight and curved, are joined, and a skin is fed into the channel and pulled through to create the tent shape. The series of arches is stabilized with interior cabling near the crown or at the eave line.

Dome tent: A geodesic shape comprised of triangular-shaped pieces. Dome sizes range from 10 to 120 feet in diameter; height proportionate.

Tent liners (ceiling or sidewall): Flexible, flame-retardant draping that covers the canopy and/or walls on the inside of a tent; can be prefab to fit a particular size and style or custom to match an event theme. *Velon*, a petroleum-based product that can be printed on, and convention taffeta are the two most common fabrications.

Pole wrap/pole cover: Disguising the metal tent poles by wrapping them with a corresponding or complementary fabric/Velon of a color used in the tent décor.

Subfloor: A custom-built floor creating an even surface inside the tent. Can be made of Biljax flooring, hardwood, plywood, event decking, or scaffolding. Can be covered with carpet, Astroturf, dance floor, linoleum, or any other lightweight floor-covering material (heavy stone such as marble slabs not recommended).

Staging: Presentation stages, ramps, risers, stairs, bleachers, and any other riser-type element fabricated or assembled on-site to raise a portion of the floor above the main floor or from the ground level to the subfloor.

Pool covers: Scaffolding installed into a swimming pool or beams spanning the pool to create the foundation for a sturdy platform. Often used for dance floors or to expand event floor space.

Fire codes: Know the regulations before you order a tent. If you're producing an event in California, get a copy of Article 24 of the California Fire Code from your local fire marshal, and speak with the Fire Prevention Division representative of the jurisdiction issuing tent permits where your event will be held.

Credit: Sidebar from feature article "Gotcha Covered" by Ingrid E. Lundquist, CSEP; *Northern California Meetings + Events* magazine, Spring 2010.

HOTEL

PROS	CONS
Sleeping rooms	Must use on-site caterer
Meeting rooms	Must use on-site audio/visual
Reception/pre-function/green rooms	Unions
Built-in stage (sometimes)	Can't attach anything to the walls
Parking	Charge for parking
Restaurant	No control over attendees after-hours
Entertainment in the bar	
Pool, exercise equipment	
Connections with local vendors	
Electricity, HVAC	
Restrooms	
Use outside florists, bakeries, etc. (usually)	

CONVENTION OR CONFERENCE CENTER

PROS	CONS
Large flex space for meetings	Must use on-site caterer
Reception/pre-function/green rooms	Must use on-site audio/visual
Connections with local vendors	Unions

Electricity, HVAC	Must provide staging
Restrooms	Charge for parking
Use outside florists, bakeries, etc. (usually)	Separated from sleeping rooms
Efficient trained staff	Limited personal interface

PRIVATE CLUB

PROS	CONS
Seasonally decorated	Your own décor may be frowned upon
Great food and service	Sometimes not flexible
Multiple private rooms	Conflicting party at the same time
Parking	Limited use of outside vendors
Military installation: high security	Credentials/security clearance for all

TEMPORARY INSTALLATION

PROS	CONS
Special to this one event	Finding a site suitable for installation
Rooms designed to fit the event's needs	Truck access
No time spent finding site	Bring in restrooms, water
No time spent in negotiations	Build on-site kitchen

Use of any outside vendors	Parking for guests and vendors
Decorate as you please	Requires qualified production team
Mix and match tent types to create the right environment	Bring in electricity, lighting, sound, HVAC
	Permits, insurance, jurisdictions, security
	Installation expense

PLACE OF BUSINESS

PROS	CONS
Employees already on-site	Unions
Parking	Rooms are the wrong size
Restrooms, water, electricity	Rooms are spread out over a large area
Facility contracts already in place (security, catering, parking, waste)	Electricity or water inadequate
Decorate as you please	Create an interesting event space
Use of any outside vendors	Disruption to daily business

PRIVATE HOME

PROS	CONS
No obvious venue fee	Inadequate space
	Vendor access and parking
	Electrical, restrooms, anxious homeowner

UNEXPECTED VENUES

- Under a freeway
- In an airplane hangar
- Empty warehouse
- Working warehouse
- Unfinished building — topping off party
- Empty building
- Neighborhood community center
- Boat or train
- Amusement park
- Museum (car, train, women's, art)
- Library
- School
- Ballpark or stadium
- Theater
- Church
- Office building
- Parking lot
- Park
- Fairgrounds
- Pier
- Beach
- Ranch or campground
- Automobile showroom or service bays
- Winery
- Nursery or farm

SPACE CALCULATIONS (COMPILED FROM OUTSIDE SOURCES***):

EVENT set-up	Approximate square footage needed per guest
Theater style	6' — 10' per person
Cocktail Parties (stand-up)	5' — 6' per person
Cocktail Parties (some seated)	8' per person
Reception (tea type, some seated)	8' per person
Cocktail Reception	8' — 10' per person
Dinner (banquet tables)	8' per person
Dinner (oval tables)	8' per person
Dinner (rounds of 10)	10' per person
Dinner (rounds of 6, 8, 12)	12' per person
Served Dining	13' — 15' per person
Buffet Dining	15' — 18' per person
Seminar	15' — 18' per person
Classroom (chair at "penny"/ skinny table)	8' per person
Dancing	2' — 4' per person
Dining and Dancing	15' — 20' per person

Banquet Rounds (need to specify how large the rounds are: 42", 60" or 72")	8' per person
Banquet Oblong (need to specify how long the tables are: 4', 5', 6', 8', 10')	10' per person

OTHER SPACE CONSIDERATIONS

Aisles	Fire exits
Multi-function space	Green rooms
Emergency equipment	Props and decor
Electrical outlets	Type of food service and bars
Staging and rigging	Handicapped access
Dance floor	Head table

DISCLAIMER *** The purpose of the space calculation list is to show you that people disagree on the amount of space needed per person at an event. DO NOT ASSUME that Ingrid E. Lundquist, CSEP or anyone working for The Lundquist Company is in agreement with any of the numbers listed below.

The following list is compiled from a variety of sources collected over the years. Some of the results overlap, but none agree 100%.

A 60" 8-top fits in a 10-square-foot space and a 72" 10-top requires 12 square feet per table. You can fit more people in a room if you use 8-tops, but sponsorships are often sold as 10-tops.

TIPS ON AVOIDING SURPRISES:
WHAT TO ASK BEFORE RENTING A VENUE

➡ What other events are scheduled that day?

➡ Can you bring in your own vendors?

➡ Is there a monetary assessment to bring in your own vendor?

➡ Will the facility be under construction or remodel?

➡ Are the in-house vendors flexible (menu, A/V equipment)?

➡ Can you put tape on the walls or hang anything from the ceiling?

➡ Are there furnishings and tabletop options?

➡ Can you supply your own alcohol?

➡ What is the corkage fee?

➡ Is union labor required?

➡ Is private security required?

➡ Is medical or first aid always on-site?

➡ What is the required insurance coverage?

➡ Are special permits required?

➡ After-hours auto shutoff (sprinklers, light, HVAC)

➡ Confirm load-in and "strike" (exit) time

➡ Review penalties

➡ Ask about bonuses or benefits they can provide

WHO'S GOING TO DO ALL THE WORK?

Whether your event is for two guests or 2,000, you are not the only person who will have some say-so in its production. In addition to the planning committees or your client, the venue and vendors all add to the success of your event.

"People input" can come from as few as four areas to unlimited numbers of areas. Think about the Olympics and the layers of people involved in managing all of the different sports, receptions, and awards ceremonies, not to mention the sponsors and their hospitality needs, the athletes and families, and coaching staffs. Then, add to that list the people on-site managing the transportation, food and beverage, lodging, and volunteer training — and the people off-site working with the credentials, uniforms, rooming assignments, and promotional items. Not only does the Olympics production involve multiple-thousands of people, but there are probably a thousand committees.

For your event, there will typically be eight to 10 different "types" or categories of groups of people who will impact the success of your event, and multiple contacts within the category.

151

ON-SITE: DEPARTMENTS ATTACHED (USUALLY EM-PLOYED BY OR UNDER CONTRACT) TO THE SITE who are responsible for anything occurring at the site.

- Maintenance, Grounds, Operations, Housekeeping
- Administration
- Food and Beverage
- Special Events and Banquets
- Activities (i.e., golf and tennis tournaments)

PREFERRED VENDORS: PEOPLE OR COMPANIES WHO ARE NOT ATTACHED TO THE SITE as employees, but have been selected to provide services for events at the site; they are paid for services by the event producer or client.

- Event planners
- Audio/visual
- Caterers
- Beverage services
- Bakeries
- Florists
- Valet parking
- Rental and tent companies
- Props and décor
- Photographers

The bonus to using a preferred vendor is that they know the site and have a relationship with the staff. They can offer suggestions and cut through red tape that might not be as easy for a vendor unfamiliar with the site.

A second bonus of working with preferred vendors is that they have worked together before on the site and, although independent of each other as businesses as a team they work in harmony.

The downside is that they may require that you use their preferred vendors and you may not be able to use a particular caterer or planner you wish to use.

Preferred vendors are not typically confined to working for only one venue. They may be on multiple preferred vendor lists.

When selecting a venue with preferred vendors, always ask if you can bring in your own vendor — some venues will assess a fee for bringing in your own vendor.

OFF-SITE VENDORS: PEOPLE WHO YOU HAVE ENTRUSTED TO PERFORM AN ACTIVITY relating to your event, but who are not attached to the site.

- Event planners
- Audio/visual
- Caterers and bakeries
- Beverage services
- Florists
- Valet parking
- Transportation
- Rental and tent companies
- Props and décor
- Photographers

When bringing in your own vendor, always ask if they have done an event at the venue before — they might be able to offer good suggestions for your event

The list of vendors is the same as the prior list of preferred vendors because whether the vendor is preferred or independent, all the same kinds of vendors are needed to produce an event.

The bonus of being able to select your own vendor:

- More control over the budget
- Broader selection of products (quantity and quality)
- You can hire your cousin or neighbor
- Setup crew and event staff can be more reasonably priced
- Use of volunteers for key roles
- Planner has an ongoing working relationship with the vendors
- The client has a preexisting contract with a vendor, such as security, which he can use for the event
- The client can select vendors of choice

Identify the decision-maker and confirm the reach of his authority.

THE PEOPLE

Identifying the people and the roles they play in the event are essential in ensuring that the event comes off as planned.

The most direct place to start is by identifying the boss and then working your way down through the other people associated with the boss and his project.

THE BOSS: PERSON, PEOPLE, OR ENTITY WHO HAS/ HAVE ASSIGNED YOU THE TASK OF PRODUCING THE EVENT.

- Your immediate boss, if you work for a company
- The head of the company (president, CEO, owner)
- The client
- A representative of the client

Whatever persona "the boss" takes, he or she is the one who has the final approval of the project and its internal elements (entertainment, venue, food), vendors and/or budget. There is always someone above you who holds the final say-so.

Look at all the faces around the table and try to understand their particular vested interest in the event and how you, as the planner, can help them accomplish it.

THE BOSS'S PEOPLE: THE PEOPLE WHO REPRESENT THE BOSS IN MEETINGS AND IN DECISION MAKING WITH WHOM THE PLANNER INTERFACES.

- Department heads
- Event committee
- Board of directors

Even though you get the nod of approval, and in some cases a signed agreement, if it doesn't come directly from the boss, it may be invalid.

VESTED INTEREST GROUPS: WHO ARE THEY AND WHAT DO THEY WANT?

Everyone involved in the development, planning, volunteering, or any other type of participation in an event has a reason for doing so, known as a "vested interest." They are interested in the success of the project because of what it can mean to their business or them personally.

Whether it's a monetary sponsorship, in-kind partnership, helping a neighbor with an after-school sports program, or a business associate who got sick, forcing someone to fill in, the vested interest of each individual and business will add to the success of the event.

Vested interest groups include but are not limited to:
- Sponsors
- In-kind partners
- Business associates, client representatives, department heads, professional services (accountants, attorneys)
- Personal connection (board of directors, committee chair)
- Vendors and preferred vendors
- Venue, contractor who holds rights for venue service/use
- In-house event and administrative staff
- On-site event staff
- Volunteers
- Guests and attendees
- Odd man out
- THE EVENT PLANNER

Businesses and organizations participate in events because it helps their business or cause. Here are some of the most common reasons:

SPONSORS
- Sponsorship benefits as outlined in agreement
- Interaction with their audience — product display, sampling, branding
- Retaining and expanding their audience
- Building relationships with the event (owner, boss, client)
- Working with complementary sponsors and partners
- Providing an opportunity for their employees to participate in a community service
- Maintaining their share of the marketplace
- Enhancing their marketing mix

IN-KIND PARTNERS

- Partnership benefits as outlined in agreement
- Interacting with their audience — product display, sampling, branding
- Retaining and expanding their audience
- Building relationships with the event (owner, boss, client)
- Working with complementary sponsors and partners
- Providing an opportunity for their employees to participate in a community service
- Maintaining their share of the marketplace
- Enhancing their marketing mix
- Getting exposure without spending cash by using their service or product as a form of payment

BUSINESS ASSSOCIATES (THE OUTREACH DIRECTOR OR MARKETING DIRECTOR, FOR INSTANCE):

- Improving his relationship with the sponsors, partners, the audience and anyone on the planning committee (board of directors, department heads, volunteers) who impacts his job
- Opening new avenues for funding through new relationships with other sponsors
- Increasing company morale through employee participation
- Observing participation of employees on the committee
- Ensuring that the product or service is presented correctly
- Ensuring that the branding requirements are followed

WHY PEOPLE GET INVOLVED

There are a zillion reasons why people and organizations become involved in events. The sections in this book strive to unravel the reasons in an effort to provide a clearer view of the process of producing a successful event time after time. Once you have an accurate understanding of the purpose of the event, and what it means to the individuals involved, you're on your way to success.

PERSONAL CONNECTION: THE HEAD (CHAIRMAN, PRESIDENT, EXECUTIVE DIRECTOR) OF THE ORGANIZATION HAS A PERSONAL DIRECTIVE TO MAKE THE EVENT SUCCESSFUL. HIS GOAL IS TO:

- Maintain a high-profile position in the community
- Be at the forefront of important projects
- Connect with other leaders
- Fulfill a promise to another person to participate

VENDORS

- Sit at the planning table with potential new clients
- Develop a relationship with the planner to get future jobs
- Take pride in their product or service and want it to be the best it can be, and show it in the best light
- Showcase products and services to committees, as well as all of the attendees and participants

PREFERRED VENDORS

- Showcase their product or service at the particular venue or for use at another venue
- Interact with planner, who can send new business their way

VENUES

- Ensure the venue is used effectively
- Showcase a variety of sites and services the venue has to offer
- Interact with planner and other committee members, who can bring additional events to the venue

IN-HOUSE EVENT and ADMINISTRATIVE STAFF (PEOPLE WHO ARE PAID TO WORK ON PRODUCING THE EVENT PRIOR TO THE EVENT)

- Enjoy taking ownership of their tasks within the event
- Interface with people other than co-workers
- Have pride in being considered part of the planning team
- Take the opportunity to showcase their skills to their boss

ON-SITE EVENT STAFF (PEOPLE WHO WORK THE DAY OF THE EVENT)

- Get paid to work off-site
- Get overtime pay for working overtime hours
- Have pride in seeing their area of responsibility take form
- Feel a jolt of excitement from the unexpected (some thing unexpected always happens that requires action)
- Interact with volunteers and attendees
- Share their knowledge of the company or product

VOLUNTEERS (EITHER TRAINED BY THE PLANNER, THE CLIENT, OR SPONSOR)

- Act as employees paid by their company to participate in community involvement
- Support their favorite cause
- Work alongside friends and family
- Meet new people
- Achieve a sense of personal satisfaction and recognition
- Morale booster

GUESTS AND ATTENDEES: PEOPLE WHO ATTEND THE EVENT

- Event mirrors their interests
- Have a shared experience (family, spouse, children, friends)
- Be offered new information and experience
- One-time opportunity
- Price, location, time/date
- Invited by someone else, part of a group
- Source of information for future conversation
- Sometimes events provide inexpensive or free entertainment and activities

ODD MAN OUT (ON OCCASION, A PERSON OR PERSONS MAY BE INVOLVED FOR THE WRONG REASONS)

In a perfect world, you want everyone on your train going the same direction. Be watchful for people who can derail your train. They might want to:

- Use the event (such as the company picnic or holiday party) as an excuse not to complete their daily job responsibilities
- Look good, so that someone else looks bad

- Just rub elbows with higher-ups, but have no real interest in the event
- Get close to someone on the organizing committee in an effort to fulfill their own personal or business interests

---

Some reasons why people are involved in a project go against the goal of the project. You may not be able to remove these people, so keep a close eye on them

---

THE EVENT PLANNER: THE PERSON RIDING HERD OVER THE PROJECT.

The event planner is listed after all the other people involved in the success of the event for the purpose of showing just how many moving "people" parts are involved in an event. Each one of those people parts represents an element integral to the success of the event.

Event planners' purpose for being involved in the event is usually two-fold:

1) They are hired because they produce events for a living, or they volunteer or are assigned because people have told them they are good at managing events.

2) They understand details and are passionate about orchestrating all the moving parts.

The consummate event planner does not consider the event completed until all the bills are paid, thank you notes are written, and reports are submitted.

MANAGING THE MOVING "PEOPLE" PARTS

The previous example of the layers upon layers of considerations required for the Olympics, and the list of categories of people who are often involved in event production, will probably make some of you wish you had never sat down at the table or agreed to serve as event planner. Some of you will say, "I'm glad I read this book before committing." Others will say, "I'm up to the task, but there must be a way to work with all these people because events take place all the time." You're right: there is a way to work with all these people, and it's called "divide and conquer."

Think of your event as a giant jigsaw puzzle. Some people separate out all the straight-edge pieces first to create a border, and others create groups of like color and assemble within the color grouping.

DIVIDING THE EVENT INTO MANAGEABLE PARTS
1) Use the divisions inherited from the prior event director
2) Adapt from seeing how someone else did a similar job
3) Create your own divisions

Even if you think you have no idea of how to divide a major project into manageable parts, you do. Every day you are an active and passive participant in the concept of divide and conquer. Just as we discussed how everyone reports to someone else, there are also conscious and subconscious precincts that create the web in which you live. Thinking "hierarchy" will help you grasp the concept of divisions and responsibilities. Here are some resources you can use to adapt your own method of division:

THE CORPORATE LADDER
1) The boss, who makes all the final decisions, is at the top of the corporate ladder and is usually the CEO
2) Vice presidents
3) Directors and managers
4) Staff or employees

EDUCATIONAL INSTITUTION
1) Head of the university system
2) Head of an individual university
3) Department head
4) Instructors
5) Students

RELIGIOUS
1) The "Almighty" of your religion
2) International leader
3) Regional leader
4) The church's leader
5) Heads of the church committees
6) Circles, prayer groups, youth groups
7) Choir
8) Congregation

Thinking in terms of "region" is another way to grasp the concept of divisions and responsibilities. Dividing by regions or physical space creates smaller geographic areas in which to manage projects.

GROCERY STORES
- Produce
- Dairy
- Meat

- Freezer goods
- Alcohol
- Seasonal promotions
- Periodicals
- Bakery
- Floral
- Natural food
- Pharmaceuticals
- Paper products
- Sale

RETAIL CLOTHING STORES

- New purchases
- Men's/women's/children's
- Accessories
- Sleepwear
- Coats
- Athletic
- Shoes

HARDWARE STORE

- Paint
- Cleaners
- Hardware
- Plumbing
- Electrical

Thinking about your home is one of the best examples, as you are constantly organizing and functioning within the space.

YOUR HOME
- Garage
- Kitchen
- Living room or great room
- Dining room
- Bedrooms
- Craft room
- Bathroom
- Guest room

Now think about the military. If you have no direct connection to the military, recall images from movies, TV, or photographs of men in uniform standing around a big table. The table has a map and on top of the map are toy battleships, airplanes, tanks, and troops. The toys are color-coded to indicate the different participants, and long sticks are used to push the toys from one position to another.

As the commander in charge of your event, think of your event in terms of its physical space and how the activities in one area impact the activities in another. Just as the commander positions his generals in different locations, the on-site location of the key event management staff is critical. The generals need to lead their troops; the catering director needs to be near the kitchen and dining rooms, and the entertainment manager needs to be near the stage and talent.

Using a banquet as an example, the banquet captain further divides the ballroom into four quadrants with a leader for each quadrant.

A seemingly overwhelming project with hundreds of moving parts and people can become manageable by simply dividing the elements into smaller pieces.

IDENTIFYING THE PEOPLE

How you identify the people on-site will also make your event run more smoothly. Venues often provide the event director with a pin or some ornament that indicates to the venue staff that they should respond to the requests of this person.

On-site event staff can be easily identified by providing a particular item of clothing representing their job position. In a large venue, bright solid colors, preferably not what you're guessing the attendees will wear, make it easy to immediately identify event staff.

COLORS (GENERAL ASSOCIATIONS):
- **Black** — used for behind-the-scenes staff (staging, audio/visual, talent)
- **White** — medical, first aid staff
- **Red, white, and blue** will probably be worn by the attendees at a political rally, so it's best not to attire your staff in those colors
- **Pastels, yellow, and brights** — good for children's events
- **Black and white** — always looks clean but make sure the event staff looks different enough from the venue wait staff
- **Neon and tie-dye** stand out but may not be the best choice for your staff at an outdoor concert

Avoid using colors related to gangs. If you are unfamiliar with local gang colors, ask the police department.

- **Red** — the universal color for danger and excitement. As such, it is more than a bold color — it is a statement. There are reds with blue tones and reds with orange tones.

Red can easily be misinterpreted and its use should be considered wisely as it has a variety of implications, including:

- Good fortune in Asian cultures
- Bad when it signifies a gang color
- Used to indicate warning, such as stop
- Associated with danger, such as blood and dashboard caution light, and hot, as in fire and fire trucks
- Sexy as in lipstick, nail polish, and lingerie
- Adult community, as in the Zona Rosa
- Secret or confidential, as in sub rosa
- The color of confidence
- A "look at me" accent color

WHAT TO WEAR

On-site event staff needs to be comfortable, so choose a piece of apparel that suits the activity of the event staff and their location, because you want to make sure they wear the uniform. Think about purchasing event logo attire to cover them above the waist, as most people own black, tan, and/or white pants for the bottom.

In some cases, volunteers and event staff are expected to pay for their own uniforms. In most situations, the uniforms are provided as part of the event budget.

Make sure your budget allows for extra uniforms. To get the best price, you may have to order uniforms long before the event staff is hired.

If the uniform calls for the event staff person to provide a particular item (such as pants or shoes), make sure you have a predetermined solution for providing that item to those who don't already have it in their closet, or let them know before accepting the position that they will have to purchase the item with their own funds.

SAFETY FIRST: Event staff should always wear close-toed shoes

---

STYLES ON TOP: WHEN SELECTING STAFF CLOTH-ING, THINK IN TERMS OF THE STYLE OF CLOTHING THAT WILL FIT THE GREATEST VARIETY OF BODY SHAPES.

- Short-sleeve t-shirts — the most cost effective and readily available
- Windbreakers and jackets — pullover or zipper are great for outdoors
- Sweat shirts
- Polo shirts
- Vests
- Hats, visors

Check with sponsors to make sure your event staff or volunteer uniforms are different than the sponsors' uniforms or giveaways

---

STYLES ON THE BOTTOM: WHEN SELECTING CLOTH-ING FOR BELOW THE WAIST, SELECT ITEMS READILY AVAILABLE IN A VARIETY OF SIZES, OR A GENERIC LOOK, AND LET THE STAFF SUPPLY THEIR OWN.

- Basic pants or slacks; black, tan, and/or white pants.
- Jeans — the term "jean" refers to a style of pant. We know the "five-pocket jean" as the typical blue denim jean.
- If allowing the staff to wear jeans, make sure to indicate they should have no holes or ragged hems.

- Indicate if belts are required.
- Indicate if low-riding pants are acceptable or not.
- "Slacks" refers to a trouser with a front zipper, usually with side pockets.

FUNCTIONAL COSTUMES

- Coveralls or bib overalls
- Aprons
- Lab coats
- Work shirts

    Any recognizable distinctive uniform that matches your theme:
    - Diner waitress or chef
    - Pilot or flight attendant
    - Cowboy/cowgirl
    - Race car driver
    - Sports jersey
    - Bowling shirts

CLOSE-UP IDENTIFICATION

- Name tags and badges
- Lanyards (a neck chain or length of ribbon-type fabric that attaches to a badge holder)
- Wristbands
- Washable hand stamps

Event staff and volunteer uniforms, as well as tools or products that will be used at the event, offer a great in-kind partnership opportunity.

SAFETY GEAR

To ensure the quality of the equipment, goggles, gloves, masks, flashlights, and other needed safety equipment should be selected, purchased, and provided to the staff by the event producer.

THE PEOPLE IN THE GEOGRAPHIC SETTING

Now that you have an idea about who the people are and perhaps what they will wear, the next question you might be asking is, "Where am I going to put these people?"

Just as you have divided your people into groups to perform certain tasks, the space will also be divided. A bird's-eye view of the geographic setting includes parking lots and restricted access areas used by vendors and people involved in the production.

Looking at the venue from a geographic standpoint will jumpstart your decision-making process about how you will divide and manage the space physically, and the people assigned to the space.

With very large venues such as fairgrounds, aerial photos are often helpful in dividing the space. Why look at the geography of the space when you know your event will have only one stage and one food area? There are many answers: traffic flow, vendor access, safety, security, location of restrooms, and entry and exit gates. If you are using only a portion of the venue, your plan will have to include a method of dividing the space. If the space is divided and, for example, the restroom facilities are located in the area you are not renting, you'll need to order portable restrooms for your side.

If a site map or aerial photos are not available, it is a wise investment to create your own map. Someone in-house can do this with a rolling measuring device purchased for less than $50 at your local hardware store. It is also an excellent opportunity for an in-kind partnership with an architecture or engineering firm. Make sure they provide a simple line-drawing map that is compatible with your software.

Indoor venues, such as convention centers and hotels, will have site maps of the venue; many will be labeled with measurements. Some venues offer these maps electronically and in hard copy. You can easily reproduce these maps with your own software.

Your event diagrams need to be electronic, so you can adapt the diagrams to meet the needs of the people using them. The same diagram that is used to show table location for setup can be edited to show sponsor tables, or indicate centerpieces, table numbers, linen colors, and props. Because the diagrams may look similar, by printing them on different-colored paper you will be able to identify them at a glance and from a distance.

Think from large to small and create as many maps as needed to suit your event. If you begin creating the maps from the start of your planning, they will serve as roadmaps throughout the planning process and be an invaluable asset at production time.

TYPES OF SITE PLANS, DIAGRAMS, MAPS
Create what you need and give it a name you will remember and that makes sense to the people using the document.

- A master site plan — shows overview of the entire site
- Building floor plan — shows existing rooms and access
- Parade route — shows parking, staging area, odd-load area, reviewing stands, and disband area
- Area map — shows the site divided into areas (stage, expo, parking, and food)
- Tenting — shows size and of type of tents
- Furnishings — shows tables, chairs, tents, stages, bleachers, and red carpet
- Facilities — shows restrooms, hand wash stations, dumpsters, and kitchen

- AV plan — shows sound, lights, power, and HVAC
- Staff — shows locations of people at the particular area. It might even be color-coded so that the people icons match their role and provide a visual indicator of who is assigned to the location and what their responsibilities are.

Check with sponsors to make sure your event staff or volunteer uniforms are different than the sponsors' uniforms or giveaways

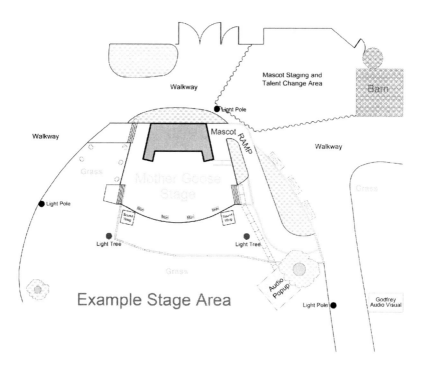

Example Event Site Plan

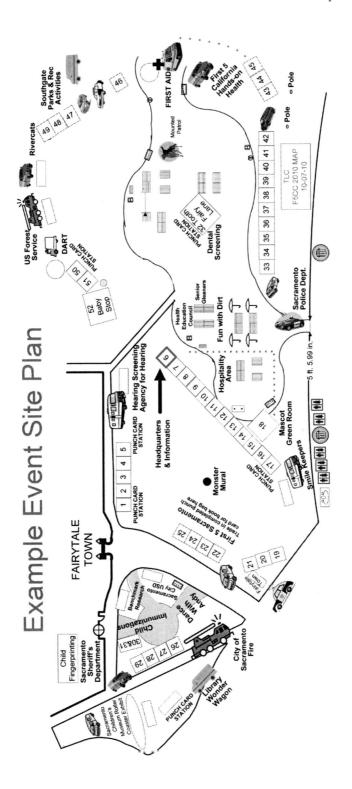

NAMING THE SPACES

After creating your basic master plan, you need to name the spaces. Some may already have names, such as a sponsored stage; others may be referred to generically, such as "over by the food area." Naming and mapping each area allows you and all staff and vendors to know exactly where everything is happening. The larger your event, the more crucial it is to have specific names attached to specific areas. The venue will have a name for the permanent areas, such as built-in stages, or a name for an area such as the Beer Garden. Decide if you will use their given or reference name or rename it for your purposes.

At Fairytale Town, a gated children's amusement park in Sacramento, their permanent outdoor "main stage" is complete with electrical, backstage storage area, stairs on both sides, and a ramp. It is called the Mother Goose Stage. When the park is rented for special events, the event producer may rename the stage for a sponsor, like "Ace Grocery Stage" or "the Mother Goose Stage sponsored by Ace Grocery." The latter is beneficial because the park already has directional signage pointing to the Mother Goose Stage.

To avoid confusion, pick a name, stick to it, and use that name in your discussions and on printed documents, including maps and vendor agreements.

ASSIGNING VOLUNTEER TASKS

After being reminded that you interface with levels of hierarchy, regional geographic divisions, and can easily identify people through uniforms, it's time to apply these concepts to your own event.

Main Stage:
- A/V
- Lighting

- Stage manager
- Stage crew
- Gatekeepers
- Dressers
- Green room
- Security

WORKING WITH VOLUNTEERS
During setup or on the day of the event is not the time to be training people. For the best rate of success, all event staff should:
- Help select the jobs they wish to perform
- Be provided with information about the event
- Be trained in advance

CREATE A VOLUNTEER JOB LIST THAT INCLUDES
- Responsibilities and tasks
- How many volunteers will be needed and the times
- (I overstaff volunteer positions by 20% and suggest volunteers come with a friend)
- Special requirements of the position (lifting or standing)

INTEGRATE A VOLUNTEER LEADER FROM THE BEGINNING
- Have a volunteer representative/s at the planning meetings
- Confirm at the onset that the volunteer coordinator involved in the planning will be the person on-board during setup and on-site for the duration of the event
- Have that person develop a list of volunteer positions based on the discussion at the planning meetings
- Set up a volunteer recruiting and reporting system

- Prepare a volunteer sheet that allows volunteers to indicate their capabilities and event experience in addition to their interest in a particular volunteer position
- Set up a system for the volunteer coordinator to communicate with the volunteers
- Have the leader train the volunteers prior to the event
- Set up a volunteer headquarters on-site

PREDETERMINE WHAT THEY WILL RECEIVE FOR THEIR EFFORTS

- Free admission tickets
- Commemorative keepsake
- Reception or recognition party

Volunteers need to be trained, uniformed, fed, given breaks, and given a responsibility they believe is personally rewarding and important to the success of the event.

AUGMENTING PROFESSIONAL AND PAID STAFF WITH VOLUNTEERS

- Create a list of positions and capabilities requirements
- Assign personality and/or traits needed to each volunteer position i.e., petite young person may be better assigned to the popcorn distribution stand than at the private talent entrance
- Overestimate by 20% the number of volunteers needed

EXAMPLE OF STAFFING NEEDS AT THE MAIN STAGE:

A/V	professional
Lighting	professional
Stage manager	paid event staff
Stage crew	paid event staff/volunteer
Dressers	volunteer
Green room	paid event staff/volunteer
Security	professional
Gatekeeper	paid event staff/volunteer

Other general volunteer categories and considerations for deciding whether the position is the right fit for a professional, paid event staff, or volunteer:

- Activities — experience and/or understanding of the activity
- Entertainment — audience expectations
- Registration — problem-solver, pleasant personality
- Information — multilingual
- Photographers — use of photos, expectations
- Food cooking — safety (cooking), speed
- Food serving — coordination, balance, experience
- Beverage, alcohol — Legal serving age
- Grab 'n' go snacks and non-alcoholic — kid-size distribution tables and containers are good for young volunteers
- Ticket takers — physical size, problem-solver
- Ticket sellers — anything involving the exchange of money should be overseen by paid staff or someone on the planning committee

- Auction display — the better it looks, the more attention it will get; this is a great task for someone who has been in retail display
- Auction spotters — think about the money; not everyone is good at this

EXISTING FACILITIES

Addressing the design and use of space in an outdoor venue was discussed first as it is more complicated because you are the architect designing and building the venue. Now that you have an understanding of the options for creating and naming spaces and identifying volunteers within those spaces, doing the same for an event taking place in an existing facility will be easy.

WHAT'S ALREADY AVAILABLE ON-SITE

An existing building used for events already has a division of rooms, running water, electricity, restrooms, parking, and either a kitchen or catering prep area. Most will have some furnishings (tables and chairs), linens, and tabletop (utensils, glasses, plates). Some facilities have basic centerpieces, like mirrors, votive candles, or bud vases to which you can add your own special touch. Other sites have entire warehouses of props and a complete floral department that can dress up your event head-to-toe.

When discussing the tabletop items available, remember to ask about table numbers and "standards," the hardware that holds the table number. Standards come in different heights and sizes. They can be ornate or plain, standing, metal bases with clips, or standing plastic sleeves.

Looking at the standards will remind you to ask about any informational signage the facility uses outside of the ballroom. Options they may have on-site could be an easel, a standard-size paper sign holder, a standing message board with changeable letters, an electronic message board, or a monitor dedicated to your event to project your video message.

Facilities usually have numbers and reserved signs that fit the standards. You will have to make signage for the tables if your tables are assigned names, are sold to sponsors, or reserved for special guests. If you have assigned seating, you'll also need a large seating chart on an easel at the registration area outside the room, and smaller copies at the registration desk.

An existing building will also have some lighting, a sound system (portable or built-in), audio/visual equipment, a lectern, draping, and skirting. If the facility has a kitchen, it may have a chef, kitchen crew and wait staff (servers), or a list of approved local caterers. Preferred or recommended vendors are already familiar with the facility and can be helpful before the event with site design for best traffic flow.

ROOM NAMES

Whether your event is indoor or outdoor, it is crucial to identify the space clearly so your guests can have a great experience and your staff, volunteers, vendors, and all other participants can easily understand the site. Room names, stage or area names, and clear diagrams and site plans will make your event easy to maneuver.

Facilities often name their rooms to reflect the location. A hotel in the mountains may have rooms named Alpine or Summit, whereas a conference center by the ocean might have rooms named Seaside and Shoreline. The good news is that the meeting or conference theme often ties into the location of the facility and the room names fit right into the theme. There will already be a site plan showing the names of the rooms, rooms will already have name signage, and the facility staff will be familiar with the room locations. The bad news is that if you're not familiar with the terminology of the area, your attendees may find the words hard to remember, such as with an event held in the desert with rooms named Saguaro and Agave.

Naming the rooms to match your event's theme means you have control over the room names, which will add to the event experience. You will also have to create new site maps and new room signage.

IDENTIFY THE INTERIOR EXISTING SPACES FOR YOUR EVENT

- Event headquarters
- Registration area
- Pre-function area — coffee, continental breakfast, breaks, afternoon refreshments, reception, book signing
- Speaker ready rooms
- Green room for talent
- Volunteer, event staff, vendor crew break room
- Event retail store
- Ballrooms — general session, meals, auction, trade show
- Breakout rooms for presentations

SPONSORS AND POSITIONING THEIR PRODUCTS

In the same sense that we discussed naming a stage after a sponsor, it's important to consider placement of their products when assigning the space at your event. What may be considered the best space to one sponsor is an undesirable location to another.

Work with your sponsor to make sure you are aware of the needs required to have their product at the event. Oil pans will probably be needed for display autos, and extra garbage receptacles for a sponsor providing a tasting.

Also, be conscious of written, implied, or understood sponsor agreements regarding competing products used and served.

Vendors who will be providing goods and services will come with their own tools of the trade. However, a sponsor or partner may request that their product be used at the event. If you have a hot sauce sponsor and are serving tacos, ask that the caterer use the sponsor's product. This will often be supplied to the caterer at no cost or at a reduced cost.

Automobile sponsors often provide the transport vehicles, and beverage sponsors often provide the beverages. Under these circumstances it is important that no other competing product be used or served on-site.

SELECTING YOUR VENDORS

After dividing your event into manageable parts, you'll see that each of the different parts has different crowd and event accommodation requirements.

The event has a band requiring a performance area (stage), and the audience needs a place to view the performance (seating).

➡ **Crowd *(seating)* and Event *(stage)* Accommodations**

The stage needs a certain amount of space, as does the audience seating, as does a changing area for the performers. In the same sense that you designed the performance and viewing area of your event site to fit the requirements of the entertainers and audience, you'll select the vendors to meet the requirements of the defined areas as well as other requirements outlined in your event plan.

It is not unusual to have several same-type vendors to accommodate the needs of your audience profiles or the locations where the product or service is needed.

IDENTIFYING NEEDS AND SELECTING VENDORS

The most straightforward way to start identifying your vendor needs is to assess the needs of each of your manageable on-site areas by checking it against the general needs for an event, which include food, shelter, restrooms, and security.

We're also including floral and parking to show examples of how what appears to be a simple line item with a simple solution can become very complicated.

Vendor selection is based on crowd and event accommodations' needs:

- Audience profile
- Size of the audience/s
- Type of service
- Event schedule
- Venue location
- Vendor areas within the venue
- On-site service requirements
- Capabilities of the vendor
- Required licenses, permits, insurance

FOOD

You may have several vendors or several types of food, price points, and types of service depending on who you're feeding, when you're feeding them and where. Here are some food service discussion items to consider:

- Sold on-site, included in cost of ticket, sponsored
- Physical setup of food service area
- Age range of the people eating
- Dietary considerations
- Ethnic considerations

- Requirements for cooking and temperature control
- Plated or bagged/boxed
- Grab 'n' go, utensils
- Disposable, recyclable
- Rented glassware and china
- Passed, served, buffet
- Sponsor product-serving requirements
- Who's being served?
  - Volunteers
  - Event staff
  - Management
  - Sponsors
  - General public
  - VIP seats
  - Handicapped

Example: Needs Assessment for FOOD for an Outdoor Event				
Outdoor festival: Setup Fri., Oct. 9			Noon — sundown	
Event day:	Sat., Oct. 10		10 a.m. — 4p.m.	
Strike:	Sat., Oct. 10		Complete by sundown	
Visitors:	5,000 — 6,000			
Staff and Volunteers: 250				
Talent	149			

Participant	Location	Time	Food	Beverage
Setup crew	Green Room	7a.m.	62 Wrapped pastries	60 Coffee
Talent	Green Room	9a.m.—4p.m.	4 Snack baskets	200 Water
Vendors	Green Room	7a.m.—4p.m.	6 Snack baskets	100 Water
Expo Booth Participants	Expo	11a.m.—1p.m.	200 Sack lunches	300 Water
Expo Staff and Volunteers	Expo	11a.m.—1p.m.	50 Sack lunches	100 Water
Attendees	Food Booths	12p.m.—4p.m.		5,000 Water
		6,000 Mini hamburgers		
		5,000 Grab and go items (raisins, string cheese, carrot packets, etc.)		5,000 Fruit smoothies
		100 Pounds of Popcorn		
		500 Apples, small red		

To ensure you cover the crowd and event accommodation needs for the entire event, treat each manageable area as an event unto itself.

SHELTER

Shelter doesn't have to mean an earthquake-reinforced bomb shelter. Shelter can be as basic as available umbrellas or a grove of trees.

Shelter simply means that you must provide a place of refuge from the elements — wind, rain, sun, snow, dust storms — whatever your guests are likely to encounter in your geographic region. Make sure you have made accommodations to keep your guests safe from expected and unexpected turns in the weather. Seating under the shelter is also a good idea, especially if it's hot.

Children can be easily accommodated without taking up a seat that might be used by an older person. Packing a few tarps, and even a roll of carpet or carpet runners, can provide clean ground level seating for the small ones. Inexpensive ponchos and light-weight, painters' drop clothes work well to cover people and product.

Barbra Riley, Photography Professor at Texas A & M University in Corpus Christi instructs her students to keep zip lock bags in their camera case, "Zip close bags have saved my camera more than once in a downpour." She also suggests being inconspicuous by carrying your camera in an insulated six-pack bag rather than a branded camera case that screams: "*I have an expensive camera inside!*"

If your audience is young or elderly and your event is outside, make sure to have plenty of shaded seating and water available throughout the venue.

A facility specifically built for large groups of people is usually an excellent place to find great examples of crowd and event accommodations. Here are some things to notice next time you're at the fairgrounds:

Close to the entrance:
- Restrooms
- Shaded sitting areas

- Food booths or directional and informational signage to the food and beverage area
- You'll feel safe within the fencing of the event site
- Uniformed security
- Signage for information, first aid, and lost and found

RESTROOMS

All venues, whether existing or temporary installations, will have guidelines for numbers of people per hour usage, depending on the type of event being held.

In an existing building, the planning department has already incorporated the numbers of people to be served into the approval of the building design and permit. However, if your event takes place outside the building or if your event takes place using temporary structures, portable restrooms will be needed.

Portable restrooms come in all shapes and sizes, from single economy units, which are delivered on flatbed trucks, to executive trailers with air conditioning, lighting, and music. There are solar units on trailers, which can be driven to remote sites. Solar units come with backup batteries. Mounted solar panels harness energy from the sun in a battery. The power is used for lighting and to activate a pump to wash your hands and flush the toilet.

There are portable restrooms with showers, often used at encampments. There are also large ADA models with handwash units, as well as freestanding hand-wash units.

Placement of restrooms is important to make sure that the crowd is served. The units usually arrive on a flatbed truck and are placed only once. Before they arrive, the event planner must walk the event grounds as if you are a guest entering the event, experiencing the event, and looking for a restroom.

By doing this you can place restrooms conveniently near all areas where visitors will be present.

A rule of thumb: place the restrooms together in groupings and make them visible to the crowd.

Restrooms can be self-contained and require no electricity, or they may require electricity for lighting and flushing. Knowing if you will be using large units requiring electricity is important for two reasons. The units are usually large, and they need to be placed either before temporary structures are built or room needs to be left to position the units after the structures are built.

The large structures are normally not used by the construction crew. Be sure to order smaller units for the construction/install crew and place them in an area that will not be seen by the guests, or arrange to have them removed after construction is complete and then returned after the event when it is time to dismantle the installation.

Placement of restrooms requiring electricity means that the source of electricity will either be brought from a main permanent building or from a generator. The distance from the main building may be too far to supply the needed electricity, and the sound or position of the generator can be noisy or inappropriately placed. These are all considerations when working with portable restrooms.

Other restroom-related topics to discuss with your vendor:
- Need for access to water
- Delivery and removal specifics, ease of moving rest rooms once placed
- Toilet paper supply
- Availability of on-site service staff
- Availability of visual screens or fencing

Some restrooms will have to be placed in specific locations, such as near or inside the green room area for the talent, near the volunteer area or headquarters for the event staff, or near the first aid area. Hand-wash units, likewise, will need to be placed by the restrooms and also at the areas of food cooking, assembly, and distribution.

The restroom supplier can provide information on numbers of people and units needed based on the profile of your event.

SECURITY

Face it, people have a need to feel safe. If they feel safe at your event, it will have a better chance of being successful because that's one less distraction for them to think about.

The security required for your event will be determined by the venue in which it is taking place and the jurisdiction/s residing over the venue. Jurisdictions include the access routes to the venue. If you are having an event that includes flight, you will be working with an air traffic controller.

Whether your event will involve land or sea, the primary jurisdiction under which your event will take place will inform you of the other jurisdictions required to be involved in the production of your event. One easy way to start identifying the jurisdictions you'll interface with is to think about the venue space, the anticipated crowd, and the planned activities at your event. Thinking about fire, medical, security, traffic, noise, and waste will indicate potential jurisdiction approval or involvement required for your event.

Example: the California State Capitol
- Building and grounds — state, California High way Patrol
- Sidewalks and streets — City of Sacramento

- Bridge over the Sacramento River one mile from the Capitol — California Department of Transportation
- Roads leading to the east side of the bridge — City of Sacramento
- Road on the west side of the bridge — City of West Sacramento
- Raley Field in West Sacramento — private property

To celebrate the groundbreaking for Raley Field, the AAA ballpark in West Sacramento, a parade was staged from the capitol to the ballpark. The parade started on city streets with the capitol in the background, but had it begun on the capitol grounds it would have been under the jurisdiction of six different entities, each with their own security, permits, insurance, and other requirements.

TYPES OF SECURITY OFTEN USED AT AN EVENT

Armed — Uniformed, usually associated with a jurisdiction. For events, police officers are often hired in twos with one vehicle. The police officers are often off-duty and serve in an auxiliary capacity.

Unarmed security — Hired, often uniformed and used for crowd control and to increase the presence of uniforms, i.e., safety at a reduced cost from armed officers.

Volunteer — Uniformed in logo attire of the event and used in low-risk areas.

Event staff — Even if they are not designated as security, the presence of event staff in event attire suggests security.

Automobile — Marked and unmarked vehicles.

Motorcycle — Usually associated with armed uniformed officers, and often used for traffic control.

Bicycle — Usually available in conjunction with a business district, volunteer, or organized group such as the Scouts or bicycle clubs.

Horses — Hired or used in daily policing of local police jurisdiction.

Dogs — Some jurisdictions do not allow dogs as part of the security, especially if children will be in the crowd.

Officers on horseback are often found in park settings and historic districts. They are used at outdoor events because officers on horseback are high off the ground and able to see further than officers on foot. Mounted patrols are able to move crowds at three times the speed of officers on foot.

THE "ILLUSION" OF SAFETY is just as important as having real officers of the law at your event and reinforces the comfort level of the crowd.

- Large safety equipment, like fire trucks, affords the fire department and ambulance services the opportunity to mingle with the community.
- Rented cherry pickers, tractors used in setup.
- Waste removal and recycle trucks.

- Trucks, helicopters, DART (drowning accident rescue team) boats.
- If your event would benefit from a fingerprinting booth, the service is provided through local law enforcement agencies by their junior auxiliary groups, young men and women who also come in uniform.
- Community-based organizations such as the library, museums, and hospitals often have large, imposing mobile units.
- In addition to the uniformed event staff, suggesting security, the presence of any group of people involved in your event (such as sponsors) in their logo attire presents a unified entity of staff, which also suggests security.

The venue you select may be under the jurisdiction of several entities, and will require approval from those jurisdictions as well as compliance with their rules and regulations.

The fence and the invisible fence are effective ways to contain the crowd and reinforce the sense of safety.

- Rental chain link fencing (as used on construction sites)
- Rental picket fencing (provided by tent companies)
- Orange snow fencing (flexible woven fencing available in hardware stores, or rented through temporary fence vendors)
- Open space (just leave acres of room between your main event and the parking lot)
- Cement barricades, crash barricades
- Bridges, roadways, structures, and natural land divisions

Example: Needs Assessment for SECURITY for an Outdoor Event		
Outdoor festival: Setup Fri., Oct 9		Noon — sundown
Event day:	Sat., Oct., 10	10 a.m. — 4 p.m.
Strike:	Sat., Oct., 10	Complete by sundown
Visitors:	5,000 — 6,000	
Staff and Volunteers: 250		
Talent	149	

Location	Time	Type	
Expo area	6 p.m. Fri. — 9 a.m., Sat.	Paid private security: Auto (1) and walking patrol; unarmed (2)	
Event Site	8 a.m. — 4 p.m., Sat.	Paid: Auto (1) and walking patrol; armed (2)	
	9 a.m. — 5 p.m., Sat.	Paid: Auto (1) and walking patrol; armed (2)	
	11 a.m. — 7 p.m., Sat.	Paid: Auto (1) and walking patrol; armed (1)	
	9 a.m. — 6 p.m., Sat.	Paid: EMT (1) with ambulance, transport vehicle	
Event Site	All day	Assigned to venue: Horse patrol	
	All day	Assigned to venue: Bicycle patrol	
	Pending availability	Demonstration at venue — pending availability: Fire truck	

Front Entrance	9 a.m. — 4 p.m.	Paid: Event staff (6)
Back Entrance	8 a.m. — 6 p.m.	Paid: Auto patrol, armed (1)
	9 a.m. — 4 p.m.	Unpaid: Volunteers (2)

When negotiating a big-name talent contract, be sure to incorporate an appearance in addition to the primary performance.

ENTERTAINMENT

For every audience type you can identify, there is a particular type of entertainment. In addition to identifying the style of music your audience will enjoy, there are also considerations such as cost, duration, and how the entertainment fits into your event.

TALENT AS THE MAIN ATTRACTION

If your event is entertainment /driven, you will select a venue to match the entertainment. A big-name star, which is expected to attract a big crowd, needs a big venue.

A big-name star could also be contracted for an event with a big budget and a smaller venue, but with a higher ticket price. When making a major investment in big-name talent, it is not unusual to add an appearance either before or after the primary appearance such as at sponsor, VIP, or employee parties.

Just as you might use your installed tent as a venue for a fundraiser prior to the main event, you might include your talent at an event preceding the main event, but for a different audience or as a teaser to the main event.

On-site considerations:
- Setup time required
- Number of band members or entourage
- Dressing room/s requirements
- Food and beverage
- Electrical requirements, lighting, sound amplification, sound equipment, projection equipment
- Hotel requirements
- Air and ground transportation requirements

The talent contract or agreement will outline the specifics of the event such as date, time, location, duration of performance, type of performance, special appearances, etc.

The rider (an addendum to your talent contract) will outline the requirements for the performer to perform. These requirements will have time, space, and monetary impact on your overall agreement.

Read your talent rider carefully — it is not unusual for the rider to be almost as costly as the performance contract

---

If the entertainment is a smaller element of your event, you can match the entertainment to the venue's available space and/or the budget. A major entertainer on stage may have a full band with an elaborate sound setup. This will take more time to both install and test than an acoustic guitar player sitting on a stool using the same standing microphone, with a boom arm, that was used by the singer before him.

A good sound technician can set your event up with an adequate sound system to suit a variety of talents acts that you have scheduled on the stage. Putting your audio/visual technician directly in contact with your talent ensures that the talent needs are understood correctly and accommodated. A non-technical person might overlook or misinterpret the performance needs.

Here's what you should consider when using one main sound system and scheduling a series of talent acts:

- Numbers of people performing
- Costume changes
- Lighting needs
- Number and types of microphones
- Sound checks
- Incorporating the electronic instruments of the talent
- Stairs or ramps to stage

FLORAL

Floral is a mainstay of an event because it comes in many varieties, shapes, and sizes, adds color and aroma, and can be a focal point or accent.

Your event will have as many floral-related vendors as you have needs. As you mentally walk through the event site, visualize where the event will need three-dimensional color. Also, think about the impact of fragrance on the guests. Very fragrant, floral displays are best suited to wide open spaces, such as reception areas, or smaller entrances that the guests will pass through quickly.

When working with major floral installations, make sure you have an available water source and adequate prep area. A floral prep area may requires temperature control, electricity, easy access to truck parking, lots of prep tables, and garbage cans as well as a green waste or yard waste can.

When thinking floral, consider the registration table, food tables (buffet or hors d'oeuvres), beverage bars, centerpieces for dining and reception tables, accents on the stage by the lectern, and specialty personal flowers for individuals. Also look for "dead space" in your venue, such as barren corners and columns.

Types of floral vendors:

- Floral arrangements
- Silk flowers
- Fresh cut bunches
- Exotic display pieces
- Trees and plants planted into the ground
- Potted plants and trees
- Rental or loaner live or silk plants and trees
- Corsages, nosegays, boutonnières, bud vases

Other floral considerations:

- Seasonal
- Fragrance
- Size
- Symbolism

RISK MANAGEMENT, PERMITS, AND INSURANCE

Often overlooked by the novice event producer are the costs associated with risk management, permits, and insurance. You may remember the obvious street-closure permit to hold your event on the street, but you might not have thought about a fire department permit for your tent. You might have thought about the insurance for the event, and missed the added insurance to have employees drive supply vehicles, or to cover the animals at your petting zoo.

Risk management is all about taking a close look at the elements of your event and uncovering any problematic situations before they occur — from slipping on a banana peel or tripping over an electrical cord to improperly cooked food and over-crowded venues.

There are ordinances, permits, and insurance for just about everything from amusement park rides and hot air balloons to fireworks and alcohol.

Walk your site, review your event elements, and ask yourself the following questions. If the answer is yes to any of them, solve the problem before it happens by talking it over with the vendor, contacting the jurisdiction you think may be in charge, and/or discussing with your insurance agent.

- Is this a problem now (low-hanging tree limb)
- Will this be a problem during setup (vendor truck parking)
- Will this be a problem on event day (crowd control/ traffic jam)
- Will this be a problem during the event (electrical cords)
- Areas that need to be secured (green rooms, financial, HQ)
- Emergency vehicle access
- Weather insurance and event cancellation insurance

My rule of thumb is, "If it requires a permit, it probably requires insurance."

COLLECTING BIDS AND PROPOSALS

After completing your "needs assessment," i.e., creating lists of crowd and event accommodations for each of the event areas, it's time to combine the needs to determine how many vendors will be required to accomplish the tasks. A spreadsheet is often the best way to approach compiling the information. Once the information is compiled, you need to find the vendor to provide the information.

As discussed earlier, some vendors come with the venue and it is required that you use them. Some venues have preferred partners, and at other venues you can use your vendors of choice. To provide information on the cost, you must provide the potential vendor with information. There are several ways to ask for information:

BID

The event planner provides a document outlining the needs and asks a selection of vendors to provide a response (including costs) from which the winning vendor is selected.

There are two types of bidding processes: open and closed. Open bids mean that anyone can submit a bid. A closed bidding system means that vendors are selected to bid. In the bidding process, some bids require that the vendors are prequalified, and sometimes certified. The process sometimes allows bids to be amended.

PROPOSAL

The event planner provides a document outlining the concept of the event and asks a selection of vendors to provide a response.

In the proposal stage, the event planner often names the dollars to be spent and is asking the vendor to provide product suggestions available for that dollar amount.

As with the bidding process, there are two types of proposals: open and closed. Open proposals mean that anyone can submit. A closed proposal means that vendors are selected to submit. In the proposal process, some proposals require that the vendors are prequalified, and sometimes certified.

The process sometimes allows bids to be amended. The proposal system does not commit that a vendor will be selected.

SOLE SOURCE

The event planner has most likely worked with a vendor before, is comfortable with the vendor's product, service, costs, and selects that vendor.

The planner provides the vendor with the pertinent information and asks for a sole source cost estimate. In establishing vendor relationships through event planning, the planner creates his/her own cadre of preferred vendors and knows their strengths and weaknesses.

Why sole source?

- The event planner can often receive a better product at the same cost or the same product at a lower cost.
- The planner already knows the extra capabilities of the vendor if last-minute product or service is required.
- The planner already knows the change order process of the vendor.
- The vendor is probably already familiar with the other vendors and they work as a team.
- Sole sourcing saves time and money.

RFQ "Request for Qualifications"

There are two RFQ's. The first is for qualifications and the second is for a quote.

The first RFQ is sent out when the planner is unfamiliar with the availability of vendors and their capabilities. It may ask for hourly rates of the people providing the service but does not ask for production cost estimates for goods and services.

The RFQ is sent out:

- If there is not a preexisting qualified vendor pool.
- If the entity wants to increase the number of vendors in the vendor pool.
- If it is required by the funding source.

RFQ "Request for Quote"

The second RFQ can be solicited whether or not the vendor has been prequalified.

The entity requesting the quote can do so in a formal or informal setting. This term is often used casually and interchangeably with the word *estimate,* as in, "Please send us a quote or estimate."

RFP "Request for Proposal"

The RFP is sent out to a prequalified vendor pool with a document outlining the event concept

Sometimes the RFP is many pages long and asks for full detailing of the event plan, timelines, names and profiles of event staff, budgets, etc. A great deal of time is spent by both the client and the event planner in preparing the RFP, responding to the RFP, and selecting the vendor to be assigned to the event. The upside is that when an RFP is involved, the contract is usually substantial. The criteria and requirements are also substantial.

The RFP may include a request for an overall budget or detailed vendor budgets; names and responsibilities of staff (sometimes staff bio's) and vendors; copies of certifications, permits, and insurance. Because the requirements can be extensive, it's best to thoroughly review the RFP before making a decision to prepare and submit a proposal.

Read the fine print. It may indicate that your primary office must have been located in a specified geographic area for a given period of time, or that companies with a particular certification receive priority status. Either can put you out of the running.

ESTIMATE

The vendor is asked to provide a cost estimate for goods and services as required from the planner.

COST INVOICED

The actual amount due for goods or services.

TERMS

The payment schedule, indicating the amount of the payments, the payments dates, and payment method.

SAMPLE FACT SHEET (NAME OF EVENT PRODUCER, DATE, PAGE NUMBER OF DOCUMENT)	
EVENT: 100TH CORPORATE ANNIVERSARY	
CLIENT/HOST: CLIENT'S COMPANY NAME	
DATE: DAY AND DATE TUESDAY, JUNE 14	TIME: START — END 6 — 9:30 PM
SITE: CLIENT FACILITY PARKING LOT; ADDRESS / DIRECTIONS:	
EST. GUEST COUNT: 400, BUSINESS ATTIRE, BY INVITATION	RSVP COUNT DATE:

AGENDA:	6 PM RECEPTION TENT; HOSTED BAR
	7:15 PM SIT DOWN DINNER; WAREHOUSE
	8:30 PM VIDEO PRESENTATION, AWARDS

ACTIVITY: HISTORICAL DISPLAY IN RECEPTION TENT

PHOTO OP (IF MEDIA COVERAGE IS DESIRED):   INTERNATIONAL GUEST SPEAKER (BIO ATTACHED); AWARDS ON STAGE; INTERVIEWS — WORK WITH MEDIA CONTACT:

MEDIA CONTACT: (MAY WORK FOR THE PLANNER OR CLIENT)   PHONE   EMAIL   EVENT CONTACT: (MAY WORK FOR THE PLANNER OR CLIENT)   PHONE   EMAIL

FACT SHEET

The fact sheet includes the facts of who, what, when, where, why, and how, plus some limited information on special activities or guests.

It also has contact information for the designated contact and ticket purchase information, if it is a ticketed event. Fact sheets should be provided to everyone working on the event to ensure the information provided to guests, vendors, media, and any other interested parties is consistent.

CREATING AN RFP

The RFP is a glorified fact sheet with specific information directed to a specific event need for product or type of service.

When selecting from more than one vendor, make sure you have provided a fact sheet or RFQ outlining the requirements so that the vendors will all be responding to the same request.

Beyond the who, what, when, where, why, and how - there is no perfect formula for identifying the information to include on your fact sheets or RFPs. Plan on developing the style that works best for you.

Without "getting into the weeds," a phrase often used by PR Consultant Nancy Pearl, you need to have enough of the basic information about the event on your fact sheet so that you can retool the document to create other event documents. When you feel like you're starting to get into the weeds, a.k.a. the minutia, it's time to start another document.

Notice how we reused the top half of the fact sheet to create the foundation of the catering RFP. The vendor list provides and agenda information that will help the caterer in determining time requirements and coordinating with other vendors during load in and setup.

Providing the vendors with as much pertinent information as possible (in writing) saves a great deal of time you would spend repeating the information later, and wondering if you forgot to tell one of the vendors something critical to the event.

Two words of caution — *information overload*. Be careful not to provide so much detailed information that they will be overwhelmed and won't read past the first page.

Color-coding documents can be used as a safety net. You can easily look across the conference table or to the far end of the event site and see if everyone is working off the same document.

Diagrams with icons are also valuable tools when you find that too many words just complicate the issue. You need to park five cars and a truck in a row, and you want the truck in position number two on the west side of the line — the images of cars, a truck, and sun will be understood by who-ever positions the cars. Providing lists, instead of pages of sentences, is also effective.

SAMPLE Request for Proposal, Off-Site Catering   page 1 of 2
(Name of event producer, date, page number of document)

EVENT: 100th Corporate Anniversary

CLIENT/HOST: Client's company name

DATE: Day and date Tuesday, June 14	TIME: Start — end 6 — 9:30 p.m.

SITE: Parking lot of client facility; Address and directions: Truck access to catering area; private catering area prep size TBD; running water available; caterer to provide electrical needs; waste removal contracted with venue; dumpsters on-site; caterer to provide trash cans

EST. GUEST COUNT: 400, business attire, by invitation only	RSVP COUNT DATE: 10 days pri-or to event

THEME:	50th Anniversary (corporate)
COLORS:	Primary color ivory Secondary color chocolate Primary accent color gold Secondary accent burgundy or crimson
OTHER	Client wants his product (chocolate) in-corporated into menu; will post recipes on corporate website; chocolates and recipes in guest gift bag

BEVERAGE:	Under separate contract
FURNISH-INGS and TABLETOP:	The event producer will contract for all furnishings and tabletop, glassware, china, flatware, linens, tables, chairs, tents, and décor, etc. Catering to provide quantities.
DÉCOR:	Provided by event producer, including catering stations and bar areas, as needed.

SAMPLE **Request for Proposal, Off-Site Catering** page 2 of 2 (Name of event producer, date, page number of document)	
BUDGET:	$_____ per person, incl. tax, gratuity, all staffing, setup charges.
SAMPLING:	6 — 8 people at caterer's kitchen; date TBD
SITE INSPECTION:	Two meetings at event site prior to event. Caterer to indicate space needed for prep area and service stations.
PORPOSAL DUE:	Day of the week _____ Time _____ Method (electronic, hard copy, fax) If by mail include address and addressee.
SELECTION:	Date and method of announcing winning proposal
QUESTIONS:	Name of contact person and method of contacting

AGENDA for _____ event. Date____. Time _____	
Contact person _____ method of contact _____	
AGENDA:	6 p.m. — 7 p.m. Reception tent; parking lot; setup noon
	NOTE: we expect the day to be hot, plan on refreshing choices Beverage under separate contract
	Passed hors d'oeuvres, finger food; five per person
	7 — 7:15 p.m., transition from tent to warehouse
	7:15 p.m. Sit down dinner; warehouse Wine and glassware TBD Protein with a mole sauce; seasonal vegetable and starch DO NOT pre-set salads; Clear table when finished; Dessert, citrus with chocolate garnish Start serving desserts at 8:10 p.m. Offer coffee and tea
	8:30 p.m. Presentation and video; stay seated
	9:30 p.m. presentation complete
	12 midnight strike complete

VENDOR LIST for _____ event. Date____. Time _____
Contact person _____ method of contact _____

Beverage vendor, hosted bar

Floral: registration table, bars

Plant rentals: on stage

A/V: pre-event montage; video presentation after dinner

Staging: size TBD, skirted, indigo back drape

Lighting: TBD, stage, dining tables, reception tent, entry area

Special effects: confetti champagne bottle from stage after dinner

Props: historical display in reception tent

Furnishings: reception — tall cocktail tables, some folding chairs at perimeter of tent dinner: tables 60" rounds for 8, dark walnut Chiavari chairs, gold cushions, no chair back covers; napkins and linen fabric and color TBD)

Restrooms: executive trailer, access between reception tent and warehouse

Valet parking

UNCOVERING HIDDEN COSTS

RIDERS

Riders are the addendum to talent contracts. They spell out the requirements for the talent to perform. Whether the performance is a solo acoustic guitar, a singer, an author reading from his new book, or a full setup stage production, the costs associated are separate from the performance fee. It is not unusual for the rider to be as costly as, or more costly than, the performance contract. Here are some examples:

- Travel
  - Air — first-class seats for performer and band or entourage
  - Land — private limousines
  - Rental vehicles
  - Parking for performers' vehicles
- Security
  - Private unarmed or armed police
  - Vehicles
- Venue
  - Back or entrance
  - Amenities — shower, mirrors, sitting area
  - Easy access from outside to inside
- Green room
  - Food and beverage
  - Amenities — shower, mirrors, sitting area
- Lodging
  - Specific types of rooms with specific amenities
- Food and beverage
  - Specific (often brand-specific) to hotel room and green room

- Audio/visual
  - Sound equipment and lighting
- Staging
  - Stools, lecterns and podiums, visual screens
- Entourage and their accommodations
  - Performers' business associates and families
  - Concierge services and tour guides
- Secondary special appearances
- Insurance, permits
  - All of the above

REHEARSALS

Performance rehearsals are usually scheduled along with the performance schedule. Rehearsals give the performers the opportunity to test the stage and the technicians the opportunity to test the sound and lighting and special effects.

If the performers do not arrive on time for the rehearsal, this impacts the time schedule of the stage crew. It may put them into overtime, or limit their time available to make any needed adjustments after the rehearsal.

It is not unusual for a speaker to forego the opportunity to experience the stage and the venue prior to the performance. For some speakers, this keeps their experience with the audience experience fresh. The sound and lighting technicians, however, may have to make adjustments during the actual performance.

A "like-stature" stand-in enables you to not only pre-test the lighting and amplification, but also the height of the lectern, podium, stools, and other furnishings on the stage.

Using a stand-in (of like stature) during setup for the rehearsal eliminates some of the preliminary unknown factors, such as lighting to follow a performer moving across the stage or the sound volume to hear in the rear of the venue. If the performance involves multiple talent, provide like-stature stand- ins for each performer.

Some performers prefer to experience the venue before a performance from the audience's perspective. You may find them testing the seats in the house as someone else rehearses on stage.

Non-professional talent, such as board members presenting awards, can be both experienced and inexperienced.

Use stand-ins during rehearsal to pre-test the staging mistakes that could occur during the performance.

Always order an extra handheld microphone, as non-professional talent often forgets to turn the microphone off or leaves it in the wrong place for the next speaker.

SAVING MONEY AND SPENDING WISELY

The easiest way to save money is to spend less or acquire the goods or services at a lesser cost. Here are some questions to ask before making your decisions about the best choice for your event.

VOLUME PURCHASE

Most goods are packaged in units. The unit will contain two or more of the same product. The units are then packaged in larger containers such as bags or boxes. Some items, such as novelty Hawaiian leis, may be simply packaged in a large box.

Buying in "bulk" refers to purchasing an item in quantity.

Usually the case or bulk price of any item is less than the cost of the item purchased individually or by the unit. If you need 100 pieces of an item, it may be less expensive per piece if your purchase a case of 144. Ask these packaging questions before making your purchase decisions.

- How the items are packaged
- How many pieces are in the case
- At what levels (number of items) the discounts occur

SHIPPING

Sometimes it is less costly to pay full price and purchase an item locally than to order the item at a discount and have it shipped.

➡ Free shipping
➡ Shipping options (land/air, regular/expedited)
➡ Out-of-stock orders may require you to change your shipping speed for the goods to arrive on time

DELIVERY

In comparing vendors, check their costs per item (tents, furnishings) against their costs for delivery. Some deliveries are from truck to door (sidewalk/warehouse bay/driveway) only, and a separate provider needs to get the ordered item through the door and to its proper location. Ask how the vendor charges, and if there are charges for delivery at a particular time or to a particular place.

1) By the mile from the warehouse to the location
2) By a flat rate per driving region — predetermined by warehouse
3) By the time of day items are required to arrive on-site
4) Time block (specific window of time)
5) Install or strike before or after normal working hours or on weekend

Further questions to ask:

6) Will there be a credit to your account if the delivery is late?
7) Will there be extra charges for:
    a. Venues on dirt roads or on hills?
    b. Venue requiring the use of elevators?
    c. Venues with stairs?
    d. Union labor?

SETUP

Setup requires labor and, often, union labor. It may be more cost effective to pay a rental company to set up their own equipment, such as tables and chairs, than to try to round up volunteers, or even your paid event staff, to set the furnishings.

If the setup is not completed by a particular time, it can impact other vendors and event staff. Example: linens cannot be "dropped" (opened/placed) on tables if the tables aren't open and set up; likewise, tables and chairs cannot be set up if the venue isn't ready to accept the furnishings, such as if they are still laying carpet, installing tenting, or removing the rentals from the event previously held in the same space.

If the event is held at an existing site, such as a conference center or hotel, your contract should name the time the venue will be ready for your installation. It should also name the start and end time available for installation without additional charges for extra security or after hours supervision by venue staff.

Ask if there are charges for setup complete at a particular time or circumstance:

1) By the item
2) By a flat rate for the job
3) Moving furnishings after initial placement

4) By the time of day, i.e., after-hours installation

5) Time block (specific window of time)

Further questions to ask:

1) Will there be a credit to your account if the setup is late?

2) Will there be extra charges for:

3) Venues on dirt roads or on hills?

4) Venue requiring the use of elevators?

5) Venues with stairs?

6) Union labor?

7) Ask if a site or room plan is required prior to the event.

8) How do they handle damaged rental items?

9) How do they handle counting rental items?

10) Do they provide extra rental items?

11) Can volunteers or event staff assist in setup?

INDUSTRY DISCOUNTS

This may be your first attempt at producing an event, but if you do a good job, you may find yourself producing more.

The benefit of being responsible for producing more than one event is that you develop relationships along the way. Building relationships with vendors is key to getting your project done efficiently and as outlined in your plan. After that relationship is built, industry discounts follow. Here are some attributes of event planners and vendors that they appreciate about each other:

VENDORS ENJOY WORKING WITH PLANNERS WHO

- Are experienced and know what they're doing
- Understand and speak their language
- Respect their expertise
- Are compassionate about their situation
- Provide food and beverage
- Function in a win-win situation
- Pay their bills on time
- Review their order in detail, and don't order items after the truck has left the warehouse
- Don't expect miracles at the last minute
- Do expect to be charged, and to pay without grumbling, if they ask for a last-minute miracle.

PLANNERS ENJOY WORKING WITH VENDORS WHO

- Are experienced and know what they're doing
- Bring the correct product
- Have friendly, appropriately dressed staff
- Understand and speak their language
- Respect their expertise
- Are compassionate to their situation
- Appreciate the provided food and beverage
- Function in a win-win situation
- Solve problems on-site
- Charge fairly
- Try to accommodate last-minute additions or changes to the order
- Work as a partner in the event-planning process

TYPES OF INDUSTRY DISCOUNTS YOU MIGHT SEE:

- Credit on your account
- Extra product
- Waived or reduced charges

Work with your vendors - a bonus to good vender-planner relationships is the opportunity for either to bring the other into an event situation that is beneficial to all involved

---

HOW MUCH WILL IT COST?

Just as we looked at the big pieces of the project while creating the event plan, the largest budget line items will probably be obvious and should be addressed first. The top line items are not always in the same order. For instance, special circumstances may make an expensive venue available at no cost to a member; to showcase in front of a particular group of people, a caterer may reduce their charges for a nonprofit organization's fundraiser; an entertainer may perform for free at his cousin's wedding; or a designer may reduce his fees in exchange for professional photographs. There are a million reasons why there is no one set budget item that is always at the top.

IDENTIFYING MAJOR BUDGET LINE ITEMS

From a financial perspective, there are four items that are usually the largest, and should be considered first: venue, food and beverage, entertainment, and décor. From the "gotta-have-it" perspective of a particular client, a very expensive invitation, a production team based in different countries, and world-renowned photographers may be at the top of that client's list.

Whatever element of the event is at the top of your client's list of what indicates a successful event should be the first item you price out and include in the budget. It may be very expensive. It may be inexpensive, but come with high shipping costs. It may cost the same as a like item but requires time to special order.

BUDGET LINE ITEM

A budget line item is an item with a separate associated cost. A budget category may be "catering," but one line item may be "volunteer food" and another "specialty dessert." Look at the list below and notice how the line items elements make up a category.

Client's "gotta-have-it" (general or specific)
- A wine bar
- 2008 Sobon Estates ReZerve®Primotivo, Shenandoah Valley, Gold Metal
- 2008 Far Niente Estate Bottled Cave Collection Chardonnay, Napa Valley

Catering — food and beverage
- Volunteer
- Staff

Venue
- Prefunction area - lobby
- Ceremony - ballroom

Entertainment
- Reception
- Dancing after dinner

COMPARING VENDOR PRICES IS MORE THAN COMPARING FOOD COSTS

A comparison isn't a true comparison unless you're comparing like items. When you create the document from which the vendors will prepare their estimate or bid, supply as much detailed information as possible and give the same document to all interested vendors.

If the document allows for questions, provide an email address to ensure that the question is in writing and that you can provide a response to the question to all vendors. Some clients hold a mandatory pre-bid meeting to address the questions of interested vendors.

When the estimates arrive, be sure to log them with the time and date. I prefer to wait for all estimates to be in prior to reading any to keep the information fresh in my mind. If the RFB is complicated, create a tally sheet, so that you can judge the entry as you read it.

Bids coming in after the deadline are an indication that the vendor does not perform tasks in a timely manner or does not take deadlines seriously. If the vendor says he was too busy to get it done on time, will that mean he's too busy to effectively provide service at your event? If there is an honest reason why the bid is late, as a courtesy to the other vendors, the late vendor should be docked points if you're using a point judging system.

Bids coming in prior to the deadline and presented in a clean, orderly, easy-to-read format will stand out from the others. These indicate that the vendor knows how to follow instructions and wants your business.

Somewhere between the early submissions and the late submissions are the exactly-on-time submissions. These are often pulled together at the last minute and missing pertinent information. The vendor is focusing on the deadline and hoping to have the opportunity to adjust his submission during the pre-award discussion phase of the process.

The more clearly you can describe your expectations, the more likely your vendors are to meet them.

VENDOR QUALIFICATIONS AND CERTIFICATIONS

Before reading any of the bids, review to make sure the vendor has provided the required qualification documents, which may include:

- Business licenses
- Driver's license
- Insurance (office, on-site, automobile)
- Food and beverage licenses and permits
- Payroll tax documents
- Financial documents

PREQUALIFIED VENDORS

When working in government or corporate situations, vendors are often required to submit documents to a central clearing house or department.

When they have passed the guidelines of being a vendor, they are assigned a vendor number. Depending on the size and type of entity you work for, your RFP may request only their vendor number as opposed to their complete documentation.

Reading between the lines:

Sometimes it's not what the bid states but what can be read between the lines, what is presented as additional service, or what is overlooked that can be the telling sign between the selection of one vendor over another.

Using catering as an example, here are some items that may not be in your RFB, but will often be mentioned in the vendor's bid:

- Tastings — not required in the RFP, but some clients and committees feel that tastings are imperative, whereas others rely on past experience or references
- Florals on buffets — some caterers automatically include these and build the cost into the overall cost; others consider it an add-on or part of the florist's bid
- Vendor provide the numbers of service staff
- Vendor provides a bid per your request and then makes suggestions for adding value or trimming costs
- Vendor will provide complimentary coffee and snacks for the event setup crew
- Vendor will provide meals for production crew
- Vendor will provide some linens at no extra charge

BUILDING THE BUDGET

Gleaning information from your needs assessment documents has provided the requirements for your event by area.

If your client or boss wants to know how much is being spent on a specific category, such as food (no matter where it will be served or to whom), simply reshuffle the papers into new budget categories. If you don't have someone managing the accounting aspect of the project and you don't use accounting software, this process can be easily created on a spreadsheet.

Working by category, here's what it might look like. Notice that the "line" indicates the amount and cost of the "items," hence "line item" budget. Line-item budgets may show columns for the number of pieces and amount per piece along with formulas to calculate the totals. We have left those columns out due to space restrictions; however, use of formulas is suggested, as they allow you to change one cell of information and, if the formulas are applied correctly, other cells in the document will change along with the single change.

PLANNER — CLIENT — VENDOR RELATIONSHIP

As the planner, you are the conduit between the client and the vendor. Be cautious of vendors who try to work directly with your client because it can impact your budget. You are the person who should make the decision to set up an extra table, and you are the one who knows if you have ordered the extra linen to put on the table. Avoid these changes unless your client agrees in advance to cover added vendor charges for additional product ordered. Clients can become caught up in the moment and regret spontaneous decisions later.

Keep your eyes open and your ears alert. Hearing your client say, "More champagne," is usually an indication that the budget is about to go up, and buyer's remorse may set in later.

Sample Event

LINE-ITEM BUDGET (Production Contract $87,000)

	EST.	ACTUAL
MANAGEMENT		
Event Master Plan (Event Overview, Marketing Plan, Timeline, meetings, creative concept)	6,500	7,150
Event Production (Production Schedule; vendor negotiation and management; on-site)	7,500	8,300
Admin. Staff	2,500	2,675
Materials — TBD		
Insurance, producer; (city is self-insured)	400	500
TOTAL MANAGEMENT	16,900	18,625
AUDIO/VISUAL		
Audio/Visual & 2 Stages	6,900	6,900
Communications	450	450
Staging (incl. wheelchair, yellow jacket at entry)	3,600	2,700
Graphics post-event	1,500	1,250
Printing post-event (15 copies Project Review) TBD	785	750
TOTAL AUDIO/VISUAL	13,235	12,050

CATERING

WATER

5,000 bottles	5,000	5,000

HAMBURGERS/VEGGIE BURGERS & CHIPS

1,500 servings @ $9.25 BBQ on-site	13,875	18,500

DESSERT

(100 dozen) 1,200 1/4 lb. cookies in cellophane with logo label & bow (RC to supply labels)	2,500	2,500
TOTAL CATERING	21,375	26,000

MARKETING

Giveaways 1,000 @$10 (several items totaling $10)	10,000	
Sunglasses		
Flashlight key chains 500@ 1.00		500
Frisbees 1,000 @ .50		500
Recycle shopping bags 1,000 @ 1.00		1,000
Noise makers 500 @ .50		250
Shakers 750 @ 1.00		750
Marketing - Professional organizations awards entries		
TOTAL MARKETING	10,000	3,000

PHOTOGRAPHER

Photographer	1,200	1,200
Documentary Photographer	600	600
TOTAL PHOTOGRAPHER	1,800	1,800

PROPS and DÉCOR

Balloons	500	825
Shakers	500	1,500
Centerpieces	1,875	1,500
TOTAL PROPS AND DÉCOR	**2,875**	**3,825**

RENTAL

Tables 22 @ $55	1,210	1,210
Chairs 250 @ $5	1,250	1,250
Linens 28 @ $9.50	265	265
TOTAL RENTAL	**2,725**	**2,725**

SECURITY

Day of	325	325
Overnight	125	125
TOTAL SECURITY	**450**	**450**

SITE

Stage	6,100		5,893
Tent	3,500		3,811
Other (permits and use fees)	50	124	
TOTAL SITE	**9,650**	**9,827**	

STAFF

Casual Labor	1,800	1,920
Event Staff 16 @ 6 hrs x $15.00	1,440	1,440
Senior Event Staff 60 hrs @ $65	3,900	4,160
TOTAL STAFF	**7,140**	**7,520**

TALENT & ENTERTAINMENT

Bands (3) @ $100	300	300
Dancers (1) Troupe @ $100	100	100
Cheerleaders (1) Squad @ $100	100	100
Clowns (2) for 3 hrs	250	250
Color Guard	100	100
TOTAL TALENT & ENTERTAIN-MENT	850	850
	87,000	86,672

You don't always need all of the detailed expense information. Here's the summary of that same budget.

Sample Event

SUMMARY BUDGET

Production contract: $87,000

NOTE: All estimates include tax, delivery, setup, and removal.

	EST.	ACTUAL
MANAGEMENT	16,900	18,625
AUDIO/VISUAL	13,235	12,050
CATERING (guest count increased from 1,500 to 2,000)	21,375	26,000
MARKETING (gift bags included items from other departments' budgets)	10,000	3,000
PHOTOGRAPHER	1,800	1,800

PROPS and DÉCOR (RWB shakers ordered for all gift bags - Fourth of July)	2,875	3,825
RENTAL	2,725	2,725
SECURITY	450	450
SITE	9,650	9,827
STAFF	7,140	7,520
TALENT & ENTERTAINMENT	850	850
	87,000	86,672

Budget numbers can easily turn into a profit and loss statement, as shown below for the same sample event.

Sample Event

PROFIT & LOSS — INCOME STATEMENT

Income		
Event Planning/ Management	86,672.00	
Total Event Income		86,672.00
EVENT EXPENSES		
Audio/Visual	12,050.00	
Catering (food & beverage)	26,000.00	
Marketing	3,000.00	
Photographer	1,800.00	
Props and Décor	3,825.00	
Rental (tables, chairs, linens)	2,725.00	
Security	450.00	
Site	9,827.00	
Staff	7,520.00	

Talent & Entertainment	850.00	
	68,047.00	
Total EVENT EXPENSES		68,047.00
Net Income		18,625.00

FLOW CHART AND CHECK REGISTER

A check register serves as a flow chart to track your expenditures.

Sample Company: Flow Chart & Check Register

Event Checking Account

Date	CK #	Acct #	Payee/Memo	Checks	Balance
2010			Opening Balance		100.00
1-1		001	Client ABC Co.		+ 21,750.00
					21,850.00
			25% Deposit		
1-2	6501	210	Hotel	500.00	21,350.00
			Site Deposit		
3-3	6502	410	Local jurisdiction	124.00	21,226.00
			Permit		
4-25	6503	252	Party Town	3,000.00	18,226.00
			Centerpieces & Shakers		
5-2		001	Client ABC Co.		.. +74,776.00.
			65% Progress Payment		
5-5	6504	290	Trading Company	3,000.00	71,776.00
			Giveaway Items		
5-6	6505	220	Audio/Visual Experts	10,050.00	61,726.00
			A/V Event Costs		
7-1	6506	210	Carousel City	5,893.00	55,833.00
	6506	211	Stage & Tent	3,310.00	
7-1	6507	231	Classy Rentals	2,460.00	50,063.00
	6507	232	Linens, chairs, tables	265.00	
7-1	6508	287	Cookie Crumbs	2,500.00	47,298.00
			Wrapped cookies		

7-7	6509	250	Balloons R Us	825.00	46,473.00
			Balloon Arches		
7-7	6510	287	Fast & Fresh Catering	23,500.00	22,973.00
			"Water/Burgers/Chips"		
7-7	6511	151	Shawn Smith	1,200.00	21,773.00
			Photographer		
7-7	6512	151	Jennifer Noel	600.00	21,173.00
			Documentary Photographer		
7-7	6513	277	Men In Black	450.00	20,723.00
			Security		
7-7	6514	281	Kern High School Band	100.00	20,623.00
			Entertainment		
7-7	6515	281	Funky Music Band	100.00	20,523.00
			Entertainment		
7-7	6516	281	Jazz Big Band	100.00	20,423.00
			Entertainment		
7-7	6517	281	Fancy Feet Dance Co	100.00	20,323.00
			Entertainment		
7-7	6518	281	Kern High Cheer Squad	100.00	20,223.00
			Entertainment		
7-7	6519	281	Chipper the Clown	125.00	20,098.00
			Entertainment		
7-7	6520	281	Rosey the Clown	125.00	19,973.00
			Entertainment		
7-7	6521	281	Home Town Color Guard	100.00	19,873.00
			Entertainment		
7-7	6522	124	Des Wright	2,080.00	17,793.00
			Senior Staff		
7-7	6523	124	Carol Carter	2,080.00	15,713.00
			Senior Staff		
7-7	6524	130	Christy Nagle	240.00	15,473.00
			Casual Labor		
7-7	6525	130	Justin Higgs	240.00	15,233.00
			Casual Labor		
7-7	6526	130	Bryson Borklund	240.00	14,993.00
			Casual Labor		
7-7	6527	130	Peyton Kennedy	240.00	14,753.00
			Casual Labor		
7-7	6528	130	Presley Hill	240.00	14,513.00
			Casual Labor		

7-7	6529	130	Dirk Knight Casual Labor	240.00	14,273.00
7-7	6530	130	Kiley Cartwright Casual Labor	240.00	14,033.00
7-7	6531	130	Jenna Brody Casual Labor	240.00	13,793.00
7-7	6532	131	Melissa Jordon Event Staff	90.00	13,703.00
7-7	6533	131	Carry Warrne Event Staff	90.00	13,613.00
7-7	6534	131	Alex Riggens Event Staff	90.00	13,523.00
7-7	6535	131	Mike Smith Event Staff	90.00	13,433.00
7-7	6536	131	Evan Smith Event Staff	90.00	13,343.00
7-7	6537	131	Jean Smith Event Staff	90.00	13,253.00
7-7	6538	131	Aly Hodge Event Staff	90.00	13,163.00
7 7	6539	131	Gabby Fathy Event Staff	90.00	13,073.00
7 7	6540	131	Leah Fathy Event Staff	90.00	12,983.00
7 7	6541	131	Connor Wright Event Staff	90.00	12,893.00
7 7	6542	131	Gavin Wait Event Staff	90.00	12,803.00
7 7	6543	131	Keley Rosenberg Event Staff	90.00	12,713.00
7 7	6544	131	Shay Marshak Event Staff	90.00	12,623.00
7 7	6545	131	Debbie Rayback Event Staff	90.00	12,533.00
7 7	6546	131	Kelly Allison Event Staff	90.00	12,443.00
7 7	6547	131	Carrie Wombach Event Staff	90.00	12,353.00
7 15	6548	220	Audio/Visual Experts "Post-Event Graphics"	2,000.00	10,353.00

7-28		001	Client ABC Co.	+8372.00	
7- 30					18,725.00
8-1	6549		Planner fees	18,625.00	
		001	Sample Company		100.00

CHART OF ACCOUNTS

The chart of accounts is a list of divisions into which your expenditures might fall. A chart of accounts allows you to indicate the category of your expenditures at the time you write the check. It then allows you to sort the checks by account number to easily check amounts spent in each account.

Your financial department or accounting office will already have a chart of accounts that they use, or you can prepare one yourself. Your chart of accounts should be only as detailed as needed to provide the end information you wish to see.

SAMPLE EVENT

CHART OF ACCOUNTS

INCOME
1	Fees
10	Staffing/Labor
20	Product Sales
30	Sales Tax
40	Ticket Sales
50	Rental Charges (Props)
60	Parking
70	Interest
80	Commissions
90	In-Kind Donations

EXPENSES

100	ADMINISTRATION		
110	Staff		
120		TLC staff	
121			Accounting
122			Administrative
123			Graphic
124			Management
130		Temporary staff	
131			Paid staff uniforms
140		Volunteer staff	
141			Volunteer uniforms
150		Professional staff	
151			Photographer
152			Videographer
153			Graphics
154			Computer
160		Training	
161			Professional
162			Volunteer
170	Communications		
171		Office	
172			Phone
173			Cell phone
174			Fax
175			Delivery charges
176			Postage
177			Photocopy
178			Reproduction
180		On-site	
181			Cell phones
182			Walkie-talkies
190			Computer equipment
191			Hardware
192			Software
200	COORDINATION		
205	Vendors		
210		Site	
211			Tent

212		Facility
213		Private
214		Public
215		Power
220		Audio/Visual
221		Sound
222		Light
223		Rental, i.e., lectern
225		Staging
226		Risers
227		Pipe and Drape
228		Rigging
230		Furnishing
231		Tables and Chairs
232		Linens
233		Flatware
234		Crystal and China
235		Restrooms
236		Guest
237		Staff
238		Incidentals
240	Waste	
241		Removal
242		Recycle
243		Daily cleaning
250	Props and Décor	
251		Rental
252		Purchase
253		Expendables
255	Floral and Landscaping	
256		Cut
257		Live
258		Silk
259		Rental
260	Transportation	
261		Tickets
262		Rental
263	Lodging	
265	Parking	

266		Valet
267		Rental space
270	Emergency Services	
271		Ambulance, Paramedic
272		First aid
275	Security	
276		Armed
277		Unarmed
280	Entertainment	
281		Talent
282		Activities
283		Riders
284		Gratuity
285		Catering
286	Food	
287	Beverage	
288	Gratuity	
290	Gifts, awards, prizes	
295	Graphics	
296		Design
297		Printing
298		Signage
300	MARKETING	
310	Advertising	
311	Print	
312	Broadcast	
313	Electronic	
314	Services	
315	Co-Op	
320	Public Relations	
321	Promotions and Contests	
322	Event Publicity	
323	Merchandise	
324	Services	
325	Sponsorship	
400	LEGAL	
410	Permits and Licenses	

420	Legal service fees
430	Contributions
500	RISK MANAGEMENT
510	Insurance - Business
511	Commercial General Liability
512	Comprehensive General Liability
520	Insurance - event
521	Weather
522	Riders
	Special circumstance (cancellation, animals, fire-
523	works, cars, weather)

TRACKING EXPENDITURES

Tracking expenditures is painless if you have consistent updated documentation at your fingertips, and you log the appropriate information on the documentation. Contracts and commitments (orders) serve as the source documents for your financial reports. A running expense log and check register are the primary sources of financial information.

CONTRACT

A contract is a signed voluntary agreement that defines the exchange of goods and/or services between the seller (the vendor) and the buyer (the planner or client). It should contain the following elements:

1) **Competency of the people signing the contract** — are they of sound mind, and do they have the authority to sign the contract?

2) **Voluntary mutual agreement** — both parties voluntarily agree to the information as presented

3) **Terms of agreement** — names the goods or services and the cost of same

4) **Offer** — one party agrees to provide the goods or services
5) **Acceptance** — the other party agrees to pay
6) **Legality of subject matter** — the terms are legal and enforceable

---

Read, reread, and understand the clause in your contract that discusses payment and termination

---

COMMITMENT

A verbal, written, email, or other communication indicating that one party agrees to provide goods or services, and the other party agrees to pay.

This is a less structured agreement that does not require signatures by both parties. In the event industry, commitment usually has a value of less than $500, such as local talent acts, organizations providing setup or cleanup crews, or specialty items, such as a cake or balloon cluster.

To ensure that every commitment is remembered, create a generic order form naming the requirements of the agreement:

- Vendor contract information
- Date, time, delivery location
- Description of item ordered
- Price and payment agreement

RUNNING LOG

Without the use of elaborate accounting software, the most efficient way to track expenditures is to enter the individual expenses into a spreadsheet and create a running log.

The running log is comprised of the dollars associated with both your commitments and signed contracts. You need to include both of these sets of numbers because your signed contracts obligate you to pay as agreed upon, and with your less formal commitment (verbal, email, mail) you have given your approval for a vendor to provide a service, whether or not it has a written and signed contract.

Entering all contractual and commitment obligations into a running log is a way to keep track of cost of the event, even though the monies have not actually been spent.

Always keep finances for one event separate from finances for another event

---

CHECK REGISTER

Monies for each event should be kept separate. Some contracts require that a separate bank account exist for their event, and some make no requirement.

As a professional, it is expected that you will manage the money provided for an event as if it were your own. Whether you treat it as an individual project in your business accounting software or open a new bank account, you must be able to provide complete financial documentation to the client upon request.

At The Lundquist Company, we have several accounts designated for events and assign each new event to one of the rotating empty event bank accounts. If all of the accounts are being used, we open a new account. This system ensures that money designated for one event is not mixed with monies belonging to another project.

By keeping your payables up-to-date, the check register will provide the current balance in the accounts assigned to each event. Dollars appearing in the event accounts will not be the same as the dollars contracted and committed, as the contracts and commitments reflect payments in full and the bank account check register shows payments and deposits to date.

DISSECTING AND REVISING THE PLAN

The client has the full budget for the event usually by one of two methods: a "not to exceed" dollar amount, or a "required specific elements" from which the dollar amount will be identified. Your needs assessment led to the creation of the budget line items divided by categories best suited to your event or your client's request.

After the largest financial contracts and agreements are made, enter the dollar amounts into the budget line items. To make the budget and running log interchangeable, simply create several financial columns next to the line item. For simplified purposes, the columns can be labeled "estimate" (purple), "deposit" (green), "balance" (red), and "total" (black). Color code the columns and insert numbers accordingly. The first numbers inserted will be contracts under "total" black.

The blank columns will show you the line items that can be adjusted, and determine whether you are on track with your proposed expenses, or if you are high or low in areas. Chances are you have overspent on some line items. The reason for this is usually because that specific line item is a requirement of the event, such as a particular entertainer, the venue, security, transportation, or a special dessert. Now you have to figure out how to stay within your budget and still provide the goods or services without jeopardizing the integrity of the event.

Here is an example of a budget in trouble. After the first chart is the solution discovered by looking at the event from a different perspective.

PROBLEM — OVER BUDGET #1

Business annual dinner total budget: $100,000

Objective:
Supply food and beverage, setup for 1,000

Original line item:	per head	Steak dinner incl. all décor, beverage, furnishings	99	99,000

Objective: Park guests cars

Original line item:	Valet parking	four hours minimum	200	800

Objective: Escorts to help people down the stairs from dinner to dessert reception area

Original line item:	Escorts	four hours minimum	125	500

		100,300
	BUDGET	100,000
	OVER BUDGET	300

Here is a solution to the budget in trouble discovered by looking at the event from a different perspective. The same objectives were met, and the integrity of the event was retained, by discovering a creative solution.

CREATIVE SOLUTION — ON BUDGET #1

Business annual dinner total budget: $100,000				
Objective: supply food and beverage, setup for 1,000				
Original line item:	per head	Steak dinner incl. all décor, beverage, furnishings	99	99,000
Objective: Park guests cars				
Adjusted line item:	Valet parking	four hours minimum	200	800
NOTE: Valet parkers work only at the beginning and end of the event, and they are appropriately dressed for this event. Make arrangements with the owner of the valet company to have parkers move to the stairs at hour two and assist guests as they move from dinner to dessert area. Have cash ready to tip parkers for extra service.				
New line item	Gratuity	tip 10 valet parkers @$20 cash		200
Objective: escorts to help people down the stairs from dinner to dessert reception area				
Original line item:	Escorts	four hours minimum	0	0
				100,000
		BUDGET		100,000
		OVER/UNDER BUDGET		0

Finding financial solutions starts by taking a look at the line items from a different perspective.

CREATIVE FINANCING IN EVENTS:
To acquire goods and services using nontraditional methods of financial reimbursement or adjusting normal methods of providing goods and services.

When you think in terms of "creative," the design element of the event most often comes to mind, but it is the creativity in the financial area of the event that can make the planner shine in the eyes of the client.

As you follow the development of the event budget, sooner or later, your client may realize that the budget is inadequate, yet he still wants the elements originally discussed. When you can see that the event is going over budget, the key to providing the original event concept within the stated budget is to review all of the elements from a different perspective. Earlier in the book we talked about opposites and opportunities — here's where some of that creative thinking comes into play in the "anything goes" field of events.

Examples include:
- A once-formal fundraiser in which the guests are now invited to come as they are and eat hot dogs.
- Dinners reconfigured into breakfast events
- Off-site events held on-site
- Four-day events shortened to two-day events
- Out-of-town conferences held within driving distance

STRETCHING RENTAL BUDGETS

Reassigning line-item costs can result in big impact, while retaining the integrity of your vision. Working with a seasoned expert in the rental industry enables you to provide your client the high-dollar look they want with a smaller budget. Every season, the rental industry brings in new product to attract or match the desires of the clientele who rents it. Professional designers travel the world, read fashion and architectural magazines, scour hardware stores and garage sales, watch movies, and interface with creative people.

Professional event designers are at the forefront of what's happening in the world of events, and they are a stable client of the rental industry. This is fortunate because rental companies need to stock what they wish to rent. I say fortunately, because now anyone can walk into a rental showroom and rent what the professional designers rent. Even for a professional designer, it is almost impossible to exactly copy an event design or tabletop. Simply by changing a napkin fold, choice of glassware, or eliminating a dessert spoon, the design becomes new unto itself.

Through the cash inventory of rental companies, you can retool a design concept to make it your own. Most rental companies have showrooms with tables on which you, or they, will test your table setting by selecting linens, glassware, china, and flatware. Showing the rental expert your vision by assembling product from their displays on your test tables will enable them to offer cost-saving solutions to attain a similar look without the expense.

Specialty linens instantly "upscale" your event

SPECIALTY LINENS

Want that WOW factor of color and texture — specialty linens are your answer.

Linens are no longer considered merely table coverings; they are the foundation of your event's tablescape — the ground on which your theme is constructed. Adding a little to your standard linen budget for specialty linens will make a huge difference on your table.

For a really tight budget, order the specialty linens and use standard napkins, or if you know your table cover will be hidden by china, glassware, centerpieces, and assorted other objects, use a standard linen and incorporate folded specialty napkins as part of your décor statement, rather than a hand-wiping afterthought.

LIGHTING

You can make an impact even on a tight budget, e.g., pin spot the cake, landscape up-lighting, a "gobo" (cut-out pattern which, when placed over a light beam, creates a projected image) on the dance floor.

The wedding cake is usually a focal point at a wedding, but lighting can be effective on any display object, such as a large floral poster or painting on an easel, or on a fountain.

Assigning part of the budget to one spectacular element rather than many smaller filler props, and spotlighting that one element, creates a bold statement.

More is not always better — drawing attention to one spectacular focal point adds pizzazz and reduces expenditures on unnecessary décor.

ILLUMINATED OBJECTS

Fiber optic and LED lighting has changed the way the designers add accents to the event. Spectacular effects can be attained by using illuminated objects.

Rental companies offer a variety of functional acrylic furniture, such as coffee tables, bars, and multi-purpose cubes that are lit from within. Canned up-lighting enables the color of the light beam to be easily changed to match the color palate of the event by changing the gel.

Glowing from within, inflatable décor comes in every size and shape imaginable and makes a dramatic statement floating in a pool, hanging from a tree, or as a colonnade to the event entrance. Inflatables are also used to attract or direct traffic. They add light to a dark area and serve double duty when branded with a sponsor or event logo.

CHINA

Even with white china, mix up shapes for a unique look. The event industry is experiencing an exciting time of growth when it comes to the selection of dinnerware readily available in inventory. Matching plates and glasses are no longer the rule when setting a table.

Today's designer takes advantage of the broad rental inventory available. The event consultant assigned to you will not only set sample tables for you and your guests to see and experience, but will walk you through their warehouse where stacks of inventory are bound to spark unique new tabletop ideas.

Mix it up — matching plates and glasses are no longer the rule when setting a table.

CHAIRS

Chair options are exciting and ever-changing. Many clients want expensive ballroom-style chairs for formal events. Wood folding chairs now come in many colors, from the standard white and black to wood tones of mahogany, walnut, and natural, to the primary colors — all of which can bring your theme to life. Colored chairs frame the table and enhance the color palate at one-third the cost of high-end seating.

Chairs need clothes too. Solid-color or patterned chair pads add that extra flare and finished look to your table. Chair covers and chair back covers dress up your chair for the formal event. Anything that can be attached to a chair can change its appearance instantly. Just be aware that it may be time consuming. Be cautious if using fresh flowers, as they can wilt quickly in high temperatures.

Adding décor to the chair back transforms the chair from functional furniture to a visual prop.

GLASSWARE

Glassware is functional and decorative. Use standard glassware at the bar and upgrade the table glasses. The purpose of a reception or cocktail hour is to mix and mingle, and to get comfortable in the event space.

The time is often spent talking in groups and moving from one group to another. Guests are more likely to examine a wine glass while sitting stationary at the dinner table in conversation with the person to their right than they are when walking around during the pre-function.

Invest your glassware money where it will be seen and appreciated.

FLATWARE

There are many options with stainless steel flatware instead of silver. The variety of utensils available enables the planner to really stretch his or her budget. The fact is that at an event, guests are much more interested in getting the food in their mouths than they are reading the stamp on the back of the fork.

Planners of parties where people read the sterling forger's stamp are probably not concerned with the rental cost of the flatware.

Expect stainless steel to cost 20% less than silver.

CONNECTIONS

The relationships you build with your rental companies are crucial. A seasoned rental consultant has the ability to help you shave costs off your budget, while providing expert advice. They have connections to other rental companies, and can often find or reproduce a product you are unable to locate.

A good vendor relationship is like having a personal backup plan that is ready to go into motion at a moment's notice. If the showroom doesn't provide enough inspiration, ask (nicely) for a private tour of the warehouse where inspiration is abundant.

SECTION EIGHT: IMPLEMENTATION

PUTTING THE PLAN IN MOTION

"The devil is in the details" holds true with the ability to successfully plan and produce an event. In this section, the keyword is *implementation*. Now that you have the event plan, identified your vendors, and sent out and collected paperwork, it's time to organize the people and the paper. What's needed? More paper... or at least more electronic documents to keep you focused.

Seriously consider your decision when tempted to use the latest version of a software program, or to try a new program you think might expedite a task. It's nearly impossible to estimate the time and energy involved in learning new software — even when you know its predecessor inside out. The best time to test new products is when you're not up against deadlines.

MANAGING THE DETAILS

If it didn't have a zillion details, it wouldn't be an event. It's not unusual to hear the words detailed-oriented, type-A, and even the word persnickety when speaking of event planners. That's probably why their events go well. These professionals instinctively pay attention to details. Every planner will have his own way of managing the details and it will change with experience, the project team that has been assembled, and technology.

PAPER OR PAPERLESS

Technology allows us to communicate instantly and create documentation in great abundance.

Unfortunately, some people create documentation for the purpose of creating documentation. Everyone is busy, and we simply don't have the time to reread documentation in search of edited information.

Although software programs allow edits to be viewed on documents, unless everyone viewing the document is at the same level of proficiency in the software program, it is not a good idea to share documents in the event setting. By sharing documents, you are expecting the other party to be in your mind and view the information in the same manner as yourself.

Somewhere during the document exchange process, you will be surprised to find out that the reader in fact did not understand what your edit meant, so glazed right over it. You assumed the edit was understood. It wasn't. Was it important? Maybe it was really important and now it's lost.

Too much paper, too much repetition, too many updated documents can clutter the message to the point of being unrecognizable.

TAKING OWNERSHIP

The easy solution to limiting the onslaught of needless documents is to take ownership. You have already identified the people in charge of areas of your event either onsite or in the planning process; these are the people who each have a primary task in the production of the event. These are the people comprising the event team who need to take ownership of their particular document. It's fine for the primary person to submit the document for review by other team members who it directly impacts, but it is not necessary to submit it to all team members for review.

The reviewed document with edit changes can be distributed in a packet of information at the committee meeting to ensure that all committee members have the complete documentation. Most likely, many of the committee members will want the documentation, but will never read through it unless it pertains to them, and those people have already seen it.

Who initiates the document and who reviews for changes? The person in the primary position on the org chart responsible for that particular element of the event.

ORG (ORGANIZATIONAL) CHART

The org chart is a document indicating the organizational structure of the people on the planning team. It may also indicate departments involved in the planning team, which in turn would have another org chart indicating who is in charge of which part of the planning process.

When planning an event at a place of business, the facility operations person would be on the planning team org chart in charge of facility use. Each team leader will have tasks and people responsible to complete the tasks. The person serving as operations team leader would also be on the facility ops org chart as the leader designating people to accomplish the facility tasks required to produce the event.

Org Chart for on-site corporate event

Planning team:
Food and beverage, entertainment, staffing,

Communications team:
Graphics, invitations, media, RSVP

Facility operations team:
Lights, sprinklers, HVAC, entry and exit doors, waste management

Management team:
Finance, legal, permitting, security

FLOW CHART

A flow chart is a diagram indicating how a process works; a sequence of events that must take place in order to get from the beginning of the task to the completed task.

Sometimes the process allows one forward step at a time; sometimes multiple actions need to take place simultaneously.

In choosing a venue, an understanding of the event is required before you can identify potential spaces. The information you need will be found in your project profile. Here's a simplified example of site selection.

➜ Estimated attendee count ➜ activities of the event (conference with breakout rooms, food, entertainment, theater, indoor/outdoor, kitchen facilities) ➜ proximity to airport or downtown ➜ parking ➜ site inspections ➜ approval (financial, permit, insurance, security) ➨ short list of venues that meet the criteria ➨ venue review (pros and cons) ➨ final selection

In the case of selecting a caterer for an event, the number of attendees would have to be determined and the type of food, venue location, and a list of potential vendors created, before an RFP could be prepared and distributed and the caterer selected.

Guest count ➨ venue ➨ food type ➨ caterers ➨ RFP

TIMELINE

A timeline begins when the project starts and outlines the highlights of activities that will take place during the coming months.

The timeline can encompass several years. The tasks become more specific as the project ramps up to event day. The timeline is a like a skeleton for the event as it shows just a basic chronological outline of the steps required to produce the event.

<u>Holiday Party Timeline</u>

January - select planning committee
February - venue site inspections and selection
March - research caterers
April - contract with caterer, talent and entertainment
May - create guest list, confirm guest speaker
June - submit ideas to graphics department
July - coordinate rentals with event theme
August - order giveaways, reconfirm guest speaker
September - contract florist and caterer

October - contract valet parking, mail invitations

November - schedule event crew, reconfirm
          all vendors, talent, and entertainment

December - finalize guests' RSVP numbers with caterer and
          furnishings, install décor. Event day.

TASK LIST

As you work your way down the timeline, tasks and dead-lines will begin to surface. A spreadsheet is often used to track the tasks, progress, person responsible, and dead-line. The spreadsheet is either managed by one person or interactive, and is as complicated or simple as required to track the progress of the event tasks.

Committee Meeting Feb. 12. Holiday event Sat, Dec. 11				
TEAM	TASK	ASSIGNED	DUE	UPDATE
Planning	Venue selection	Sally Smith	Feb 15	Short list
Planning	Caterer	Sally Smith	Apr 28	Ongoing
Comm.	Invitation copy	Cindy Jones	June 20	Done
Comm.	Graphics	Bill Tailor	June 20	Three concepts done
Comm.	Select graphic concept	Cindy Jones	June 24	In review
Facility	Reset HVAC	John Clark	48 hrs prior to event 12/7	On calendar
Facility	Window wash	Steve White	24 hrs prior to event 12/8	Monthly wash —schedule changed

Facility	Amplified sound approval	John Clark		Done
Mgmnt.	Talent contracts	Joanne Ott	Apr 28	Pending
Mgmnt.	Sat. (weekend) security	Tim Miller	Apr 28	Added to contract

PRODUCTION SCHEDULE

A detailed line-by-line list of people, places, and activities taking place at particular times from the install through the strike is called a production schedule.

The production schedule is arranged in chronological order and starts when the first event staff sets foot on the venue, and finishes when the last person leaves and the venue is returned to the pre-event condition.

This document will be many pages long and is overseen by a "line producer" or production manager who worked on the development of the budget and has first-hand knowledge of the vendors, their contracts, and timing. The person assigned tracks the line items as they occur. The production schedule can list the activity and location of every vendor, staff person, sponsor, entertainer, security, etc.

If a vendor, entertainer, or staff person is performing one task in the morning and another in the afternoon, the production schedule will indicate the change in activity and location.

Always include plenty of buffer time in your production schedule to allow for traffic, security checks, and other unexpected activities that might impact your timing.

The production schedule is also a tracking tool to schedule and record time of vendor activity to ensure it matches the vendor agreement, or impose a fine or bonus as outlined in the agreement.

As the production schedule develops, be sure to indicate the most current date of changes. The production schedule is reviewed line-by-line by the planning team to ensure that all elements of the event are included. Changes or additions are made. Print the final production schedule close to the event date to make sure you have included as many last-minute changes as possible. Distribute final production schedules to the planning team prior to the event and have extra copies available at the stage.

EXAMPLE:

There is only one truck-size parking space at the venue. The catering truck is scheduled to arrive at 5:00 a.m., unload, and move to the overflow parking area by 6:30 a.m. The furnishings rental truck is scheduled to arrive and park at 6:45 a.m., unload, and move to overflow parking by 7:45 a.m. It's 7:00 a.m. ,.. and the catering truck is still in the unload parking space. The furnishings rental truck cannot unload. The caterers can be fined if there is a provision in the contract. When one entity throws off the schedule, it can impact the entire event's timing and cause general unrest.

Printing the final production schedule on colored paper is a good way to see, from a distance on event day, that all involved are working from the proper document.

AGENDA

A brief outline of the activities taking place during the event is called an agenda. It is often used as a reference document in meetings, and events involving food service.

DINNER AGENDA	
2:00 p.m.	Room set with tables and chairs
	A/V set up and tested
4:00 p.m.	Linens dropped
	Florals delivered, large installed
	Tables dress, centerpieces
4:30 p.m.	Registration table set in lobby
	Ice sculpture delivered, installed
5:30 p.m.	Guest registration
	Cocktail hour, reception
6:40 p.m.	Invocation
	Food service; coffee on request
7:25 p.m.	Presentation
8:00 p.m.	Award Ceremony
9:00 p.m.	Event over
11:00 p.m.	Strike complete
BREAKFAST EXAMPLE	
6:00 a.m.	Setup
6:30 a.m.	Coffee station open for event staff
7:00 a.m.	Tables dressed, registration table in lobby
7:30 a.m.	Guests arrive
8:00 a.m.	Food service
8:45 a.m.	Presentation
10:00 a.m.	Event over
11:00 a.m.	Strike complete

SCHEDULE OF EVENTS

A schedule of events is brief list of activities to take place during the event. On an event flyer, the activities may be listed with times and bullet points or included in the graphic bubbles or in promotional copy. The amount and kind of information you provide is related to information such as the name value of the talent, and whether the event is free or ticketed. Big-name talent with name recognition has less need of explanation.

In your media materials, on-site program, or on your web site, you can list as much information as you think will be required to provide the reader with the understanding he or she needs to make a decision about attending the activity. Location, time, photos, bio, and ticket price should be included, especially if you have an event in which some activities are free and some ticketed.

SCHEDULE OF EVENTS		
Generic information		
	Family activities and entertainment all day long	
Type of activities		
	Magicians, singers, dancers, stilt walkers	
Specific information about activities		
	3 p.m.	Thor the Magnificent
	4 p.m.	Sally Vincent and The Singing Cowhands
$7	2 — 6 p.m.	Barbecue fundraiser at the Chuck Wagon, benefitting the Upper Headlands chapter of the American Medical Response Association

BEO (BANQUET EVENT ORDER)

A BEO (Banquet Event Order) is a document prepared by the banquet manager, and used by the catering staff that indicates the type of food service, location, time, number of guests, and setup. The BEO also details everything pertaining to food service at a specific time in a particular location.

BEO		
Client contact information		
Grand Ballroom	Thursday	June 14
	Setup by 8 a.m.	Strike 11 a.m.
Registration	8' table by main door	
	Skirt table in black	
A/V	Wireless mic	Lectern
	Planner to bring client logo for lectern	
	No projection	
8:45 a.m.	Sound check	
Tables:	60"/8 tops	Set for 56
	Ivory drapes	
	Sage overlays	
	Sage napkins (fold flat)	
Floral	Planner to bring centerpiece and place cards	
Preset	Water in goblets with lemon slices	
	Coffee pots (regular and decaf)	
Iced tea and hot tea on request		
No bread baskets		
9 a.m.	Plated meal service	
	50 herbed chicken omelet and mushroom tart	
	6 vegetarian meals (colored tickets at place settings)	

SCRIPT

The script starts when the first person, usually a greeter or emcee, steps on the stage.

The script is timed and details the activities that will take place on the stage. The script includes the names of the people or acts on the stage and their performance time, as well as any staging needs for placing or removing furniture (such as stools and lecterns or podiums) or equipment (such as microphones).

The script also indicates the location from which the talent will enter, as well as lighting, sound, and video instructions. Special effects, such as confetti cannons or reveals, are also found on the script, as well as special cues to get the next speaker ready by the stage for his or her entrance.

The script is written in chronological order with three time indicators. The first indicates real time. Another indicator shows a block of time referring to how long a speaker or performer will take to speak or perform. The third starts with zero, when the show begins, and keeps a running time reference. Following this running time log enables the director to speed up or slow down the activities as necessary to keep within the time frame of the presentation.

The person "calling the show" is equipped with a headset, and is in communication with the other audio/visual technicians as well as the director, stage manager, and others assigned headsets. The person calling the show is an integral part of the production team because his cues serve as the eyes and ears of the production, and he verbally cues the others on headsets as to the next event to take place.

Here's an example of what his script would look like:

START	TIME	RUN TIME	INSTRUC-TIONS	TALENT	ACTIVITY
			Lights up stage left; enter Board Chair		
			Lectern mic volume up		
			Lights up on lectern; lights down stage left		
9:05	5	0		Board Chair	Welcome
					(Speech typed in here with word "end" cue, "Now join me in the Pledge of Allegiance")
			Lights down on speaker		
			Lights up on flag		
9:10	3	8			Pledge of Allegiance
			Lights up on lectern; down on flag		
9:13	2	10		Brd Chr	Intro Exec Dir
			Lights up stage left; enter Exec Dir		
			At lectern - hand off — Board Chair to E D		
				Brd Ch	Exit stage left
			Lights down stage left after exit		
9:15	12	22		E D	Year in Review
					(Speech typed, here, "end" cue, "The video we're about to show says it all"
			Lights down on lectern		
			Lectern mic volume down		
9:37	4	26	Roll video		

CHECKLIST

Every person will probably have his or her own checklist, from the volunteer event staff who jots a note to remember to bring close-toed shoes to the on-site headquarters manager who is overseeing the venue and people within the site.

There are as many types of checklists as there are people in the world. Invest some time searching the internet to find a format you like, or simply start from scratch and design one yourself. At TLC, we custom design an event checklist for each event because by using a list from a prior event, you may overlook an element essential to this event.

As resource material, gather up the paperwork you already created on the areas at the venue. Imagine yourself going to the venue on event day or setup day. Walk yourself through your day, writing down anything you might need to take — extra pads of paper, extra batteries for your phone, a flashlight, and a chair. Next, walk through the activities you have to do. Think about the other people on the team and what they might come to you for — tape, boxes, felt pens, scissors, Velcro, extra name tags. Another important step is to imagine yourself as an attendee, vendor, talent, sponsor, client, or special guest, and walk through the event seeing it from their eyes. This will give you a start to the items on your checklist.

Finally, meet with your planning team members at the site, at the time of day your event will take place. Walk through the event again (with your drafted checklist in hand) and verbally describe how the event will unfold. Make notes of any reminders — order extra recycle cans — and add items to your checklist as you go.

Start working with your checklist as soon as it is revised after your walk through. Put the list in a staging area away from your cluttered desk and start assembling the items, marking them off as you go. Add new items and mark them off as well. After everything is assembled, return to your supply room and glance around to see if there is anything else you might need, such as tarps, rope, more garbage bags, and put these in your staging area.

Now, systematically assemble boxes, mark all sides with the name of the delivery area and general contents. If you have many boxes, color code each area, create area checklists, and number boxes.

CHECKLIST		
Main stage	10	Extra production schedules
	2	Clipboards
	6	Retractable pens — red ink
		Asst paperclips, sticky notes, stapler, index cards
Green room		Kleenex, hand cream, mints
	24	Bottled water (room temp.)
Registration		Staff name badges
		Attendee name badges
		Extra name badges/printer
		Calligraphy pens, tape binder clips, blank envelopes

STAGE LINGO

Although it is the responsibility of the show director, stage manager, and audio/visual folks to make sure the stage show goes as planned, you'll be well advised to know the basic terminology you might hear them using.

STAGE DIRECTIONS

Stage directions refer to activities and placement occurring on the stage. These will be found in the script.

- Stage left (audience right)
- Stage right (audience left)
- Upstage (toward the back)
- Downstage (toward the audience)
- Pit (orchestra area in front of stage)
- Overhead grid (where overhead lighting is hung)

BLOCKING

Blocking is the term used to provide the talent on the stage information about where they stand and move during the performance.

During rehearsals, the assistant director and stage manager develop a prompt book as a reminder of blocking decisions made during rehearsal.

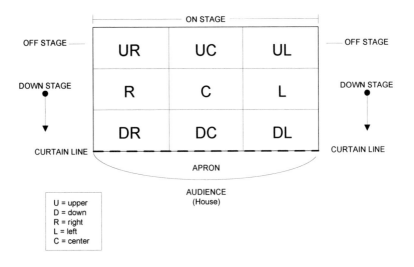

A/V TERMINOLOGY

Becoming familiar with the language of your vendors will help you more effectively communicate with them. Some audio/visual phrases appeared in the sample script. Here are more easy to understand A/V terms:

House lights up

Fade to black

Volume up or down

Standby (get ready to execute cue for lighting/audio/video playback/camera)

Go or take (execute cue or camera switch)

Roll (start video playback or record)

Set (move into position)

Strike (remove from position)

Lighting (general stage wash, "special" for a lighted area like a podium or specific prop, person, or group)

Key light (front), fill light (front), back light (back)

Backdrop (stationary drop from ceiling; move into position from side)

IT'S SHOWTIME

As the event producer, you and your production staff will primarily spend your time behind the scenes making sure that all the pieces of the event fit tightly together and that the event runs smoothly. After the event starts, leaders assigned to dedicated areas will manage their areas of responsibility, but you'll also be walking the site. You'll be keeping your eyes open for anything that looks out of place (like children in the beer garden) or a situation that might need attention (overflowing garbage cans).

If you have already mentally run though every problem that could occur, you already know the steps you will take to solve the problem. The mental exercise of problem solving is second nature to professional planners and a good one for you to start practicing. When you think you've answered that final question, look again and you'll see another hiding behind it.

BEHIND THE SCENES

The excitement really starts to become visible when all the supplies are packed, and you arrive at the venue. Depending on how well you have prepared, these few minutes and hours can be either calm and methodical or utter chaos. Order and clarity can easily be seen as normal by the client and vendors, but mayhem is like a rapidly spreading airborne virus. To ensure that your event team is in control and ready for action, arrive earlier than the client and vendors and setup headquarters in a central location. This extra time allows you to settle-in and appear as if you have everything under control.

SETTING FOOT ON-SITE

- Packing your supplies correctly makes the difference between an easy on-site setup and pandemonium. Here are some more packing tips:
- Mark boxes correctly by identifying their on-site location and contents.
- Group boxes by location when packing into the transport vehicle.
- Put the "first-needed" box in the transport vehicle last so it is the easiest to reach. This may be the box containing the master vendor list, extra production schedules, and walkie-talkies.
- Set up headquarters first. Headquarters should be in an easily accessible location.
- When selecting the headquarters location, consider the event's needs for electricity or security (locking doors).
- A centrally located headquarters is effective for a festival-type event where the headquarters will be fielding questions from the vendors and attendees.
- Make sure someone is always at headquarters and that the person has communication capabilities with the event director and area managers.
- Predetermine the activities to take place in the head quarters, and if you need a separate area for volunteer or vendor check-in, lost and found, talent check-in, etc.

MULTI-DAY INSTALLATION — WHAT TO BRING, WHAT TO DO

If the event has a multiple day setup, your vendors doing the setup will also need a headquarters area, which may have needs requirements.

- Arrange for a lunch wagon or catering.
- Order separate restrooms for the installation crew — they will not be using the same restrooms ordered for the event.
- Tables and chairs if they are not already on-site.
- Bottled water.
- Use a pop-up tent or have a tent installed if you are outdoors.
- Battery-operated lighting.
- Clothes appropriate for the weather.
- Hard hats if you are working on a construction site.
- Always wear closed-toe shoes.
- Extra charged cell phone batteries.
- Camera (or cell phone with camera) to document anything that needs to be documented.
- Ladders, step stools, and necessary hanging equipment.
- Hand trucks to move supplies.
- Paper towels, tape, scissors, felt pens, safety pins, clothespins, wipes, a basic tool kit with hammer, screwdriver, pliers, etc.

SIGNAGE

Your signage should be marked and grouped by areas and by installation time and date. A signage map indicating location and sign number should correspond with the number on the sign. There's nothing worse than having to unroll several large banners in search of the one you're looking for.

Generic signs that are to be reused should be opened at least a month prior to the event to ensure they are still in good shape and that you have enough time to replace the sign if necessary.

Before ordering any signs, make sure to check the regulations of the venue to determine how the signage can be attached to the walls or hung from the ceiling.

The venue may require that all signage be displayed on easels. Two or three easels may be included in your contract. Often, venues will rent additional easels to you for your event or you will have to add them to your furnishings rental order.

Companies that make the signs cannot be relied on to have display apparatus such as easels or standing banner holders. Check with the venue first. Some venues will require that their staff, a union member, or the staff of a preferred vendor install all signs on their property.

Venue signage requirements and installation regulations can increase your budget

---

LARGE BANNERS

Large banners requiring scissor lifts and heavy electronic billboards or monitors will likely be installed when the space is clear of vendors.

These will be first on your installation list and also on the production schedule. Some venues require that union labor be used to hang the signs. If this is the case in your event, make sure that you have allowed enough time for the union labor to complete the task.

Make sure that the person leading the sign installation team knows exactly where the sign is to be placed (height, centered above door), how it will be supported or hung (from which beam, fence, railings) and with what (rigging, rope, cable).

Methodically, signs requiring ladders are installed next, then those requiring use of step stools, and finally, signs that can be hung while standing on the ground. The exception to the rule is an area being used prior to the main event, in which case all the signage needs to be hung simultaneously.

Equally important is the manner in which the sign will be hung in the location. Hanging indoor signage has a broader "light source" window of time than an outdoor venue (after the sun sets). Outdoor venues also pose questions of temperature, which might damage signs if left out overnight. The least amount of time your signs are outside, the better shape they will be in. By installing signs outdoors the night before an event, you are running the risk of having to adjust them the next day.

If you're planning to install signage indoors after hours, make sure the lights can be manually operated so they will not turn off during your installation.

FINAL WALK-THROUGH

After the installation crews have completed the site setup, gather the vendors, client, committee, sponsors, and event staff for a final walk-through.

The final walk-through is often combined with a rehearsal, and the time is prescheduled. Start at the entrance and walk the site as the event director (explaining what will take place in the different locations) and as the attendee, simultaneously. You will notice things like missing signage, garbage cans out of place, or a new water fountain by the exit gate that was installed after you selected the venue and created your site diagram, which now may cause a foot traffic bottleneck. Having the vendors and your event staff with you allows the correct person to take responsibility for solving the problem. It is also a good way to let the people feel the experience of the event and know firsthand where everything is located.

Is it really necessary to gather all these people for a final walk-through? Yes. It can save much time and streamline the process of correcting a situation that may involve two or more entities, because they are all there to work through the solution.

This is also the time when the client may wish to add or change something. Maybe it is possible and maybe it isn't, but it's better to find out before the event starts than while the event is taking place.

The final walk-through is also a great time for those who will be on stage to have the "on stage" experience by actually walking on the stage and speaking into the microphone. A run-through or rehearsal at this time allows the sound and lighting vendors, special effects crew, and stagehands an opportunity to fine-tune using the real people, instead of stand-ins.

DAY-OF BEHIND THE SCENES

If everything has gone as planned without major incident during installation, the first early minutes of being on-site on event day are mild and even sluggish. It's simply the calm before the storm.

Being on-site before the all the event staff and vendors arrive gives the event director a few quiet moments to connect with the space. Set your mind to the "slow down" mode during this time. You need to be able to think clearly, accurately assess situations, and be able to make decisions based on the best interest of the event.

A keen ability to calmly, quickly, and effectively solve problems on-site is what separates the novice event director from the professional.

Moving fast and making snap decisions, on the other hand, can cause unnecessary mistakes, waste time, impact your budget, and result in general chaos.

Event day brings with it new people and new problems. A person with a key role is almost always stuck in traffic, the name tags didn't print out correctly, no one got change for the cash box and the banks don't open for two hours, the florist delivered the order to the wrong venue, and so on. Having a well-organized and easy-to-find headquarters offers an immediate sense of stability to the event.

During the beginning hours of the event, when the headquarters or information booth will be the busiest and the lead person needs to focus on answering the questions impacting the success of the event, position someone with the capability of instilling calm and the ability to answer basic questions at the booth to share the responsibility.

INTERFACING WITH THE EARLY BIRDS

Somehow, people once removed from the event (such as volunteers, the client's staff, booth staff, or those related to a sponsor) have a tendency to forget why they are there, where they are supposed to be, and when they are supposed to be there.

Be gentle with these people and calmly provide them with as much information as possible to make their, and your, life easier. They are important to the success of your event and it is most important to remember that they just arrived day-of and it's all new to them.

Also keep in mind, that these are the people who will report back to their boss about how well they were treated at the event.

BACKUP

People, uniforms, instructions, parking passes, credentials, name tags, clipboards, cameras, cell phones, walkie-talkies... if you are supplying volunteers or event staff with items they will be using to perform their duty at the event, always bring plenty of backup supplies.

WALKIE-TALKIES AND OTHER COMMUNICATION DEVICES

All communications devices should be tested on-site during setup. People assigned to use the devices should practice their use during the final walk-through to become familiar with the equipment and how it is properly used. Communications equipment should be provided to responsible people and used to communicate about the event during the event.

THE CARE AND FEEDING OF YOUR CAST AND CREW

One thing in particular that is appreciated by event staff and vendors is easily accessible parking. Send out parking passes accompanied by site maps and instructions well in advance of the event.

If you are asking people to arrive early in the morning, the best wisdom I can offer is to have coffee, tea, orange juice, bottled water, some pastry or bagels, and apples. This combination of food and beverage offers a selection for almost any finicky eater. Nothing is worse than a cranky vendor, committee member, event staff, or client who hasn't eaten yet.

Another food tip is to have a stash of small apples (fruit), small packets of nuts (protein), and bottled water at your event headquarters.

A designated break area, food appropriate to the time of day, and an agreed-upon understanding about timing for breaks will keep your crew happy. Make sure your first aid station is stocked with bottled water and ice. Orange juice is another good item for the first aid tent.

Your client might want to eliminate the cost of this line item, but in the big picture, the investment in feeding the vendors and production crew is your ticket to a smooth-running event.

GREEN ROOM

The talent (performers, special guests, speakers) waiting room, a.k.a. green room, will also need to be stocked with whatever is noted on the contract rider. In addition to food and beverage, there may be requests for mirrors, hand wipes, mouthwash, etc.

If there is no talent rider, providing the same basic food and beverage you have set aside for the event crew is appropriate. Multiple green rooms for different people with a stage presence may be needed, such as one for talent and one for your keynote. Stock them appropriately.

Again, if you are asking people to arrive early in the morning, supplying coffee, tea, orange juice, bottled water, some pastry or bagels, and apples is a smart move.

Breath mints are also appropriate in the green room, as is some type of protein such as small packets of nuts or string cheese.

Make sure you have indicated to whoever will be using the green room/s the policy for smoking and alcohol consumption.

SPECIAL GUESTS

Just as your talent rider will outline on-site requirements for the performer, special guests such as speakers and dignitaries will have special needs. In preparing the site for special high-profile guests, a good relationship with their contact person can be invaluable.

Special needs may include separate restrooms, separate entrances, multiple rooms for their security staff, and private rooms for meetings, media interviews, and receptions.

High-profile guests may also require a security "sweep" of the property. The sweep team is a group of security provided by the guest and often accompanied by dogs. They visit the venue and methodically move from room to room, checking all entrances and access to the facility to make sure it is safe for the guest. A detail of officers often remains on-site after the sweep and throughout the arrival and departure of the guest. Other security details may travel with the guest.

Although you will most likely be advised that a sweep will take place, or you can assume one will take place due to the profile of a special guest or speaker, you are not told when this will take place or if more than one will occur. What you can count on is that setup activity will be interrupted during the sweep. Allow extra time on your production schedule to account for the down time you anticipate resulting from a sweep. The advance team should be able to give you a rough idea of the amount of time to allot.

SETTING THE STAGE FOR PHOTOS WITH SPECIAL GUESTS

"Credentials" is a term used to mean that the individual, such as an attendee, sponsor, performer, or vendor, has been preapproved to be in special secure areas.

At some venues, such as military installations, credentials are assigned to individuals specifically. Band members, vendors, and guests cannot swap credentials, as they are usually checked against photo IDs. Military bases also require proof of registration for the vehicles.

Submit the documentation early to allow adequate time for the approval process. On-site approval is never guaranteed.

Credential requirements range from a photo ID card showing you belong to a particular organization to a name badge or backstage pass provided by the event to submission of documents that are preapproved by the entity managing the high-profile special guest.

It is not unusual to be asked to provide a passport, driver's license, company ID card, or other evidence of your stature, citizenship, or other information relevant to the particular situation. *A preapproved list is often required for a photo opportunity, attendance at a private meeting, or an interview.*

DISASTER PLAN

A disaster plan is a predetermined plan of action in case of a disaster. Disaster can range from problematic weather and equipment malfunctions to life threats and riots. The one thing disasters have in common is that they occur right now, and they are unexpected. However, if you do not have a disaster plan, and the venue does not have one in place either, having a high-profile person as a guest is a good reason to create a disaster plan.

In any disaster, it is important to know in which jurisdiction the event is being held, the closest source for medical treatment, and an exit route out of the venue. Guests will be looking to the event staff for guidance, so arm them with at least this basic information. Persons designated as management for specific areas of the venue should be provided with more information about what to do in a disaster. Chambers of commerce often provide this type of information.

Always have medical personnel at your event. A first aid tent is appropriate for festivals, and an EMT in the back of the room (out of sight) is appropriate for a formal dinner.

FOREWARNING

A forewarning is an indication that something may go wrong. A forewarning may come as easily as looking out the window, seeing the rain, and packing ponchos. It could be the nightly news showing picketers following your special guest at his last tour stop, or hearing that a freeway off ramp is closed, which means your attendees will probably be late.
The key is to address forewarnings head on.

USE YOUR SIXTH SENSE

Intuition lets you know if you feel like something might go wrong and gives you a chance to act now while you can make a difference.

Event planners have a keen sixth sense. They seem to know when the crowd will drink more lemonade and when they are in the mood to purchase logo items. A lot of this has to do with watching trends, knowing your audience, and having a keen sense of your surroundings.

Think about the profile of your event and guests and the type of activities you have planned.

Once, during setup at a golf tournament, I "sensed" a flood would occur if uphill sponsors dumped their ice out the back of their hospitality suites. I called in a carpenter and his crew to dig a canal around my client's hospitality tent, and also had them build a bridge from a supply truck to the hospitality suite's prep kitchen.

By day two, I watched the ice water pass by our tent in the canal. By day three, it was pouring rain, and because of our canal, we had the only tent with a dry-ground surface. I called the on-site catering service and asked that they deliver all the prepaid coffee and doughnuts unused by the rained-out hospitality tents, to our tent. Next, I sent our event staff out to invite everyone into our tent and we made a sign reading, "Welcome — hot coffee and doughnuts here." This sixth sense endeared my client to the other sponsors and their invited guests.

Another time, a festival site in a park was flooded with 120,000 gallons of water on a Friday afternoon after all the tents had been erected. Park maintenance was able to turn off the water, but the other park crews' workers were gone for the weekend. The site had to be ready in 15 hours and the responsibility was mine. I called a disaster/restoration cleanup company. They worked into the night, then arrived at sunrise to finish. The venue was ready to go when the vendors arrived the next morning. The cost was minor in comparison to the backlash that would have resulted from having to cancel the event or from attendees walking in mud.

There are lots of stories like these in my career and similar stories in the careers of other event planners. The interesting thing is that we consider this type of ingenuity second nature. It's only when guests and clients bring attention to an action we took that we are reminded of it. Averting crisis is an event planner's every day behavior. Solving problems and especially avoiding them before they start is what makes an event a success.

Here are some examples to start training your sixth sense:

EVENT ELEMENT	CONSIDERATION
Pyrotechnics	Fire, crowds, pickpockets
Kids outside on a sunny day	Bee stings, sunburn, scraped knees
Big name talent	Gate crashers, paparazzi, groupies
Retirement dinner	Heart attacks, choking, slip-and-fall

Family reunion picnic in a government funded gated park with entry fee	Guests don't have money for entry fee, park full, no wheel chair access to picnic site, restrooms locked

ON-SITE MANAGEMENT

Everyone reports to someone. For the purpose of simplicity, here's how the chain of command works at an event.

Every individual at an event — be it an attendee buying a ticket at the main gate, a vendor with his credential coming through the back gate, or a volunteer looking for headquarters — is connected to someone. These individuals usually have instructions specific to the job they will perform.

TEAM LEADER

Individuals may be reporting to a person referred to as a coordinator, administrator, supervisor, or any title coined by the event.

We'll refer to this person as a team leader because he or she is directly involved with individuals. There may be many team leaders in an area or working on a specific part of the event. They report to area or project managers.

AREA AND PROJECT MANAGERS

With your site divided into areas or projects, you have already identified the people who are in charge.

While on-site, these people will refer to the production schedule, agenda, stage script, or whatever other piece of documentation was prepared to track the activities in their area of responsibility. Following their list in chronological order will enable them to anticipate the next activity and be alert to situations that may need attention.

The area managers report to the event director and manage the people assigned to their area. As needed, they will assign specific tasks to their crew and may indicate leaders within their crew.

EVENT DIRECTOR

The event director is in charge of the event as a whole. He or she oversees the area and project managers. The event director knows more about the event that any other single person involved in the event. The event director relies on the management team to manage their piece of the puzzle while the event director oversees the big picture.

Qualities of an event director while on-site:

- A fine-tuned memory of how the many diverse parts fit together to make the whole event
- Eyes in the back of his or her head
- A sixth sense about risk management
- The ability to read a crowd
- The ability to foresee problematic situations
- The ability to solve problems efficiently and effectively

LINE PRODUCER AND THE LINE-ITEM BUDGET

Every event has a budget and it is usually created as a "line-item" budget, meaning that categories of expenses are identified and details of expenses follow on individual lines (see Section 7).

Creating a line-item budget makes it easy to discuss a specific item because categories are broken down into related line-item costs.

A category example would be food and beverage. The examples below show two versions of a beverage category.

Organize your budget to make it the clearest and most useful for each event you plan.

A caterer might want to organize the order by time sequence and the event director by location. Below is the same line-item information presented in two different priority listings.

EVENT DIRECTOR LINE ITEM FOOD AND BEVERAGE BUDGET					
LOCATION	TIME	BEVERAGE	COUNT	COST PER	TOTAL
Hospitality tent	Monday 8 a.m.	Coffee	50 people	3.50	175.00
Hospitality tent	Monday 2:30 p.m.	Soda	50 people	2.50	125.00
Volunteer area	Monday 8 a.m.	Coffee & water	10 people	5.00	50.00
Registration	Monday 6 a.m.	Coffee	8 people	3.50	28.00
				TOTAL	378.00

CATERING LINE ITEM FOOD AND BEVERAGE BUDGET					
TIME	LOCATION	BEVERAGE	COUNT	COST PER	TOTAL
Mon. 6am	Registration	Coffee	8 people	3.50	28.00
Mon. 8am	Hospitality tent	Coffee	50 people	3.50	175.00
Mon. 8am	Volunteer area	Coffee & water	10 people	5.00	50.00
Mon. 2:30 p.m.	Hospitality tent	Soda	50 people	2.50	125.00
				Total	378.00

The line producer develops and oversees the budget with the input of the people assigned to specific categories. All costs to produce an event are not known at the onset of the event. A draft budget will provide a good estimate, but every budget needs to be managed as the event progresses.

A cost may be increased in one area, requiring a cost decrease in another area to stay within budget. The line producer is like a watchdog over the finances, knowing where there is wiggle room to add a new line item, and where one might be deleted. He or she is also well-versed in finances, event elements, and product and service vendors. Knowledge of how the budget fits together allows the line producer to provide the same result, such as lunch, at a reduced cost by changing the type of service from a sit-down meal to a brown bag sandwich. The end result is that lunch is provided.

COLOR CODING LINE ITEMS

When everything is printed black on the paperwork, it is easy to overlook a line item. As your budget develops, color coding line items allows you to more easily spot missing line items and budget areas needing attention.

Color coding can be used before, during, and after the event. Before, colors might indicate line items that need to be completed or are completed. As the budget develops, it is helpful to identify which line items have been contracted or costs finalized. This can be done by starting out with all line items in the budget in a particular color. The color can be changed once an estimate has been received, and again when the cost is finalized.

During and after the event, the accounting or bookkeeping entity can use color coding to show deposits and final payments.

The event as a whole will have a multi-page budget. The pages will be filled with categories appropriate to the manner in which the event has been divided for accounting purposes.

A summary budget lists the totals in each of the categories. Sometimes the event requires a summary budget in addition to breakouts, such as food and beverage subtotals for volunteers, guests, and staff. The three subtotals will create the total.

Find out the format and information the client desires to glean from the event and arrange your budget to most easily present that information in a logical format.

MEASUREMENT

By the time you set foot on the event site, you have already determined what you are going to measure and how you are going to take the measurement. Your clearly marked measurement box should be packed with whatever you need to take the measurement.

MEASUREMENT SUPPLIES
- Rolls of tickets and coupons
- Cameras and extra batteries
- Wrist bands
- Passes and credentials
- Registration lists
- Envelopes of will-call tickets
- Parking passes
- Food and drink coupons
- Electronic information-capturing devices

If you're taking a survey or asking attendees to fill out a questionnaire, imagine yourself as an attendee at the event.

THE ON-SITE SURVEY-TAKER SUPPLIES
- Clipboards
- Writing instruments
- Tables and chairs
- A place for their children or spouse to sit
- Refreshments

MORE MEASUREMENT-TAKING TIPS
- Make your questionnaire short with easy-to-answer questions.
- Provide a good reason to take the time to fill out the questionnaire, such as a perk — a movie ticket, book bag, water bottle, or other benefit.
- Don't create a bottleneck by the front or exit gate.
- Let your attendees get inside and enjoy the event before stopping them to ask questions.
- Make sure you have informed your staff of the profile of the type of attendee you would like to have them interview, such as families or seniors.
- If you're interviewing vendors, schedule the interview for their off-peak times.
- Schedule the taking of surveys as well as the locations.

If your measurement involves staff or volunteers interviewing attendees, be sure to train them in the proper method of asking the questions to ensure your questionnaire provides accurate responses.

DECIDING ON SURVEY QUESTIONS
- Don't ask arbitrary questions just to report that you took a survey — ask your client and sponsors in advance what information they would like to learn.
- Match the questions to the profile of the attendees — don't ask teenagers about hearing aids.
- Ask questions requiring only a "yes" or "no" answer.

REPORTING THE SURVEY ANSWERS
- Methodically transcribe the answers and provide them to the client or sponsors.
- Review the answers to the questions and provide a summary.
- Calculate the number of responses (22 of the 25 adults surveyed said they do not drink decaffeinated cold beverages).
- Review the answers to reveal patterns (all 22 of the adults who said they do not drink decaffeinated cold beverages also said they do not drink decaffeinated hot beverages).
- Findings — the great majority of the adults surveyed don't drink decaffeinated beverages.

In advance, qualify and quantify the results expected by your client or sponsor. Hiring a professional research firm is often a worthwhile expenditure.

THE BIG FINALE

One of the biggest surprises to the first-time event planner is the length of the preparation time and effort expended before the event in comparison to the actual duration of the event. The event itself flies by when the adrenaline is rushing. Unlike the guests and attendees who exit quickly, the vendors, event staff, and finally the event director leave to take on the next conquest. How you leave is as important as the attention you paid to set up when you arrived.

STRIKE

Systematic removing the event elements and returning the site back to its pre-event state is referred to as *strike.*

You may have heard the term used in a theatrical sense, meaning to remove the props or to turn off a light. In punctuation, think of the term *strike-through,* which is to eliminate. There's also *strike* as in unrest among workers, or as in to hit or light a match. However you remember to associate the word strike, it means to remove. The *install* or set is the front end of preparing the event, and the *strike* is the back, or tear-down of the event.

Leaving a venue as clean as or cleaner than when you took control of the space does not go unnoticed by the venue or its management. If there is something you can do that will benefit your event while enhancing the venue, that's even better. After first obtaining approval, here are some ideas that will create a win-win situation for your event and the venue. Be sure to include a cost line item in your budget, or time (volunteer or staff) needed to accomplish the task.

Planning ahead will ensure that you don't take items back to the office that should have been thrown away. Order extra dumpsters and dispose of your item once.

At the end of a long event, no one wants to go back to the office or warehouse to unload. There are two solutions to this dilemma:

1) Park the vehicles in a secure place so they can be unloaded at a later time

2) Hire or assign a cleanup staff specifically to arrive toward the end of the event to manage the site cleaning, packing of supplies, delivery back to the place of origin, and replacing the supplies in their proper location. This effort is a project in itself, but it may prove to be time and money well spent, to do it now so you are fresh to take on the task of compiling the results data in an orderly manner when you return the next work day.

LEAVE THE VENUE BETTER THAN YOU FOUND IT
- Directional signage (parking, exits, restrooms)
- Informational signage (restrooms, drinking fountains, historical reference, bus schedule)
- Stripe parking lot or repaint sidewalk parking zones (red, yellow, green, blue)
- Install new garbage cans or paint old ones
- Create a professional site map

SIGN OFF ON VENDOR PICKUPS
- Have adequate staff for cleanup and strike.
- Pack disposable gloves and masks.
- If your strike includes moving heavy objects, make sure you have brute strength to do so.
- If your event includes an expo-type space in which vendors and booth participants will be, provide garbage bags, instructions, and directions to the dumpster. Periodically send someone around to the booths to ask if they need additional garbage bags.
- Reread the contract to determine whether your agreement includes paying the vendor's staff to set up and tear down tables and chairs, or just to deliver. If you are paying to just remove, your staff will have

to fold up the tables and chairs and move them to location indicated on the contract (usually the side walk, driveway, or other place easily accessible by a truck).

- Count tables, chairs, linens, and all other rental products against the order and install list.
- Check for loss and damage; indicate the same to vendor and make sure both you and the vendor sign off on agreement.

Don't feel rushed. Always count rental items and record damaged goods (photograph if possible). Your rental contract will stipulate compensation for damage and replacement.

WHAT TO PACK FOR CLEANUP

- Garbage bags (large and small)
- Zip-close bags
- Bags with handles
- Same-size boxes (like file boxes, which will stack easily — don't throw these out after you have emptied their contents)
- Disposable gloves
- Face masks (dust masks)
- Dust pan, broom, push broom
- Shovel, rake
- Scissors, matte knife, pliers
- Paper towels, spray cleaner
- Hand trucks, dollies, pushcart
- Extra visors, hats, vests, other work-related clothes
- Lots of water and some packaged food

Cleanup is a great time to involve community service by enlisting the help of a local teen group and making a donation to their organization.

CHECK OUT THE STAFF — WHEN THE EVENT STAFF ARRIVES THEY CHECK IN AND WHEN THEY LEAVE, THEY CHECK OUT

- Record hours of work time
- Return uniforms used for the event
- Return radios, walkie-talkies, flashlights, or any other device or equipment used during the event
- Sign or supply any other documentation needed for payment

CHECK OUT WITH SECURITY

- Security should be scheduled to stay until the last person leaves.
- The end of an event can attract transients, the curious, and recycle collectors — a uniformed security officer will keep them in tow.
- The officer will advise you if you will be charged for extra hours, or if an officer was released early, and then will bill accordingly.

CHECK OUT WITH THE VENUE REPRESENTATIVE

- A representative of the venue will be checking in with you throughout the event to make sure it runs smoothly. He or she will also check in at the end to inspect the status of the venue and your experience on the site.
- Now is the time you review the pickup arrangements of any items being left on-site for future pickup, such as portable toilets, dumpsters, or event production supplies.

- Return any items borrowed from the site such as dollies, hand trucks, hammers, brooms, garbage cans, and folding tables and chairs.

TAKE DOCUMENTARY PHOTOS OF THE VENUE BEFORE, DURING, AND AFTER THE EVENT.

I always thought my dad's unspoken motto was, "If it doesn't move — paint it." Mine is similar, "If it's unusual — snap a photo."

Photograph:

- Anything unusual when you arrive
- The venue filled with people (not unusual but take your own shots of something you want to document as you might see something the event photographer might miss)
- Anything unusual during the event that can be corrected for the next event, such as lines to the bath rooms and overflowing garbage cans
- Anything unusual when you leave

POST-EVENT PHOTOS

If you haven't already done so, at the end when the venue is pristine clean, take photos of the items you added to enhance the event site, such as signage, freshly painted garbage cans, or the newly striped parking lot. You should be able to pair these with the photos you took during your initial site inspection to prove that you left the venue in better shape than before your event.

If something has been damaged during your event and requires repair — take a photo of the damage, and return after it is repaired for repaired photo.

EVALUATING SUCCESS — TAKING HOME THE MEMORY

You've heard the phrase, "It's not over 'till the fat lady sings." That concept doesn't completely hold true with events. Through considerate planning and foresight, events can live indefinitely.

I use the term *considerate* in relationship to the elements that have to be considered to provide source material to document the event after it is over. If you have created collateral materials, performed a measurement, maintained a budget, collected press clippings, and/or conducted a survey, you have the business side of the source materials to start building your Project Review.

As you gather the documentation, refer back to the project profile to ensure you have included the proof of success your client wants to see. Are they interested in the quantity of new leads or the quality of the leads?

PROJECT REVIEW BASIC INCLUSIONS:
- Documentary photographs
- Executive Summary

291

- Quantitative/qualitative measurement (graphs, charts, lists)
- Media clippings and social media documentation
- Collateral, advertising, and promotion

THE IMPORTANCE OF DOCUMENTING THE GOOD, THE BAD, AND THE UGLY

By whatever name you refer to the document, the Project Review is the culmination vehicle through which you prove your results. Start by gathering and organizing all your documentation. Put photo documentation first, followed by an Executive Summary, then numbers. All the other charts, collateral, clippings, and media materials can be organized in a manner that will be logical to your client. Placing your least valuable piece of information in the very back of the book is probably a wise idea because the reader may never get to the back.

Why include information that doesn't support your goal or shows that you didn't reach your objectives — because as a professional, it's your responsibility to report the facts. Showing the bad and the ugly reinforces that the good information is factual.

NUMBERS

People are fascinated by numbers. When tallying numbers, make sure you provide accurate and honest numbers that have backup source documents.

Refer back to your original event plan showing the measurable objectives and your methods of counting. If you measured correctly, you should have more than one way of counting — number of hot dog buns used, number of food tickets collected, number of attendees through the gate. Record the totals of the numbers collected on a spreadsheet and insert comments while allowing readers to reach their own conclusion about the relationship between the numbers.

Often during the review of the numbers, you'll find an item that you had not intended to count, but was counted, or you'll see an unexpected relationship between two numbers. In a survey we took several years ago, we asked for the attendees' zip code, assuming we would record six or eight different zip codes.

The results showed the attendees had come from more than 20 zip codes, which indicated that for many attendees this event was a destination event, not a neighborhood event. We were able to use this information the following year in both our outreach efforts and sponsorship solicitation. The zip codes showed a particular sponsor, who was on the fence about participating, that the event did reach out to their target audience.

RESPONSE NUMBERS

Many clients are also fascinated with numbers as they relate to responses. These numbers show that someone has taken an action as a result of the event. Often a dollar amount can be assigned to the value of the results of your efforts.

Immediate response examples:
- Web site hits
- Phone messages
- Reply cards
- Internet hits and sharing

Media can respond to your press materials in a number of ways, which ultimately translates into your event information reaching their audience. Media responses can be measured in increments, such as column inches for print, and seconds

SAMPLE ATTENDEE MEASUREMENT

Count method	Box office clicker count inside gated venue	Event staff clicker count at entrance
Weather on event day		54 - 83
Event time		10a.m.-4p.m.
11 a.m.		511
11:30 a.m.		1,293
11:40 a.m.	1,045	
1 p.m.		3,537
2 p.m.		5,309
2:15 p.m.	4,858	
3 p.m.		6,527
Event staff clicker count at closing		6,903
Box office clicker count at closing	7,234	
AVERAGE COUNT		7,068
Additional misc. people		
Talent & parents (back door entry)		149
Expo booth staff & volunteers		250
Estimated people on-site		7,302
Raffle tickets given out (color coded)		
Children		3,086
Adults		2,855
		5,941

or minutes for broadcast. These numbers are then translated into cost of advertising dollars for the same space, time, and/ or placement.

Media response examples:
- Interviews
- Articles
- News stories

WORKING WITH PHOTOGRAPHERS

Photography is integral to documenting and measuring an event. It's discussed here, in the final chapter, rather than under "Vendors," so that it will be fresh in your mind as you finish the book. From an event perspective, photographs are the most valuable marketing tool in the event planner's toolbox. Through photographs you are able to stop time by capturing the image as it happens.

Good event photographers are cut from a different cloth. They anticipate picture-perfect moments and pre-select their best angle to snap the photo. Some are very good with close-up shots of dressed tables before the guests arrive, and some with candid crowd shots. Some have no fear of heights and can often be found in a cherry picker or atop a scissor lift. Be sure to inform your photographers what you are measuring so that they keep their eye out for a good shot in addition to those listed on your shot sheet. And, remind them to be safe in choosing their vantage point and considerate of the venue.

MEASUREMENT
- Measure quality (smiling faces, people hugging)
- Measure quantity (crowds in front of a stage, at entrance)

- Measure quality and quantity (interested attendees at sponsors' booth)

SPONSORSHIP
- Sponsorship solicitation (brochure to attract or retain sponsors for next year)
- Sponsor thank you (large format photo with plaque, autographed or personalized photo)
- Sponsor results (sponsor representatives, sponsor booth, sponsor signage)
- Sponsor pre-and post-event (inclusion in sponsor-branding, newsletters or on their web site)

VOLUNTEERS
- Volunteer (outreach vehicle to involve new entities)
- Volunteer (recruit and retain)
- Volunteer opportunities (sponsor/employee base)

PUBLIC RELATIONS
- Public relations (media kit, photo journalism, news letters, awards entries, annual reports, social media)
- Human relations (employee recognition)
- Employee motivation (activating involvement in a cause)
- Team building (management and staff working together; departments working together)

DOCUMENTATION
- Recording results (visual used for reference or to brief a new employee, sponsor, or committee member on the project)
- Acknowledgment of the project (capturing live event details)

- Planning document (reviewed when planning for the next year)
- Commemorative keepsake (limited edition coffee table book)
- Event-related book (cookbook, poetry book, how-to book)

EVENT
- Print collateral (posters, tickets, flyers, bus benches, billboards)
- Signage (pre-event at sponsor locations, on-site)
- Promotion and advertising (print, broadcast, social media, web sites, cross-promotions)

BRANDING (LOGO AND/OR PHOTO)
- Uniforms (volunteers, staff, participants)
- Collateral materials (entry forms, participation letters, invitations, playbills, tickets)
- Souvenir items (t-shirts, mugs, key chains, Frisbees, water bottles, bandanas, hats, tote bags, mouse pads, wine openers)

While creating your event plan, mark anything and everything that can be captured with a photograph. If one of the objectives is to have happy guests, you need to provide something at the event that will make the guests happy, then you need to document the happiness as it is happening.

Documentation of "happy" is best done with photographs (a still image with no sound) and videography (moving images, often with sound). Documentation with photography can also be used to capture the overall essence of the event, show sponsor products, and record images of hazards to address at your next event. Photographs are also a great way to allow the viewer to evaluate the success of an event.

SHOT SHEETS

The key to acquiring the images you'll need to show results is by creating "shot sheets" for your photographers. The shot sheets explain to the photographers where they should be, when they should be there, and what they should photograph.

In developing the shot sheets, review the event plan to make sure that your instructions will capture images of each of the objectives and hidden objectives noted in the plan. When you review the expectations with your photographer, he is likely to have additional ideas of photo opportunities that will convey the message you wish to capture.

Every event should have a minimum of two photographers. My rule of thumb is to hire as many photographers as it takes to capture the images needed to tell the entire story of the event. If you need more photographers than indicated in the budget, contact an amateur photography club or the photography department at your local college or university. These photographers-in-training will often shoot your event for free if they are allowed to use the photos to advertise their work, or they will shoot for a much lower fee per hour.

Working with amateur and professional photographers:
- Review their portfolio before hiring
- Discuss photographer's attire for the event
- Provide all photographers with official event credentials
- Provide easy-access parking passes
- Provide a rest area and food
- Provide a schedule of events and assignments
- Discuss photo requirements (from a scissor lift, on top of a building, on horseback, in a boat, in the rain or sun, indoor lighting)
- Agree on the number of photos to be shot

- Agree on the time, date, and method of delivery of photos
- Agree on distribution of photos to client, sponsors, attendees, participants (sometimes entertainers, school groups, clubs, and organizations will expect or want photos of their performance)
- Agree on whether the photographer will upload the photos to a web site for purchase and the purchase price
- Agree on duplication charges for photos
- Agree on general and specific photo usage by client and sponsors
- Ask the photographers to cull the photos to a pre defined number
- Agree on costs of photo use for purposes other than event documentary. Sometimes the client may wish to use a photo on their web site, for print or on-line publications, in a brochure, in the results documentation, or in contest entries. This may be included in the photographer's fee or charged separately.
- Assign a person with photo use/release agreements to accompany each photographer if the client's intention is to use event photos for marketing purposes. Make sure you have signed photo-use approval from persons being photographed for promotional materials.
- Some events post signs at the entrance stating that by passing through the gates attendees are agreeing to be photographed at the event. Contact a legal entity for proper wording.

CAPTURING THE MOMENT

Determine how many photographers you need by reviewing the schedule of events taking place and the location of the events. Just as you assign managers for physical areas of the event space, you'll want to do the same with photographers. First consider the abilities of the photographers. Is one better at capturing images of stage talent and another better at candid shots? If you believe the photographers are equally good at both stage shots and candid shots, start them off in one location at the beginning of the event and have them swap locations midway through the event.

There's nothing worse than sorting through several thousand photos after an event and finding out that the one shot your client wanted of him and his granddaughter is not in the mix, or that there is no shot of the client or the local elected official who came in the back door and was only on-site for five minutes. Arming your event staff with cameras and briefing them on taking snapshots can be beneficial when looking for that one image that eluded the professional photographers. The snapshot may not be perfectly framed, but it's better than missing the moment altogether.

Professional photographers are usually more prepared to capture the unanticipated moment than amateurs.

When providing your photographers with instructions on the images you want, set aside time to review the shot sheet verbally so they know exactly what you are looking for. If the photographer is unfamiliar with the venue, review the shot sheet as you walk the venue prior to the event, preferably with the other vendors who might add to the conversation. If the photographer is already familiar with the venue, you can review the shot sheet off-site with the photographer in person.

Photography tells the story of the event after the fact, which makes it very important to have the right photos. Here are some pointers when thinking about not only how to direct the photographers but what you, the event director, should be watching out for on-site.

BE CLEAR WITH YOUR INSTRUCTIONS

Once the speaker moves away from the lectern, the opportunity is lost. The instruction to "photograph the speaker on stage" is different than "photograph the speaker on stage during his speech as he's making hand gestures, and make sure you include in the frame the event logo signage on the lectern."

INTRODUCE THE PHOTOGRAPHERS TO THE CLIENT

Let the client know that the photographer is there to serve him and will check in, or hover from time to time, to see if the client has a request.

ROOM AND TABLE SETUP

The pristine room photo is another fleeting image. To get the cleanest photo, you need to capture the room when the setup is complete and before the guests have arrived. This is a brief and fleeting moment. Remind the photographers that the table needs to be completely set, not partially set (missing napkins, glasses, and centerpiece). If possible, provide a sketch of what the table will look like when completely set.

"EXPECT THE UNEXPECTED"

Surprise is good to remember when it comes to being prepared for the moment. If your event includes a confetti blast, photos of falling confetti are nice, but capturing the look on the faces in the crowd is better. Better yet, alert one of the photographers to specifically capture the expression of a special guest.

NAME BADGES

Do you really want to see name badges in your photos? If not, remove or ask your subject/guest to temporarily remove them. Some clients actually do want to the guests to leave on their name badges so they can blow up the photos after the event if they need to identify the people in the photos.

WINE GLASSES, NAPKINS, AND FOOD

Eating and drinking photos are especially important if the event is based on food and wine, but maybe not the best choice of shots for a business meeting.

LEFTOVER FOOD AND PRODUCT ARE A GREAT WAY TO "COUNT BACKWARD"

If you provided the food, you know how much you brought (cases of wine, hot dog buns, give-aways). Photograph what is left and count it later.

UNUSED DINNER NAPKINS

If you didn't provide the food, you can count the number of people fed by putting the unused napkins all on one table and taking a photo. Use the photo to count napkins later. Match your registration head count against the caterer/restaurant count with the unused napkin count.

OVERFLOWING GARBAGE

Yes, take photos of problematic situations.

CULLING THE PHOTOGRAPHS

Digital photography has made access to images immediate, and many clients expect immediacy when it comes to photos of their events. As part of the agreement with your photographers, ask them to cull out the bad shots before providing you the images. What you want to see from your photographer is a quality image — not a quantity of images.

Photographers have the eye to detect problems with a photo much more quickly than a non-trained eye. If they provide you with all the digital photos, be prepared for many long hours of culling the photos yourself. Having a disk of all the shots is good for backup if there is a particular image you're looking for that is not found in the culled photos.

PRESENTING THE RESULTS

The whole idea of producing a business event is to boost the bottom line, and you do this by designing the event to meet objectives. Now is the time to present the results in a manner that will show the event in its best light. This presentation is not about you; it's about the event and the results. Your skills will be apparent if you are able to effectively prove the results. Just as with the photographers and using the event plan to identify photos to be shot, use the event plan as a checklist to create your presentation.

The results should be presented in the manner agreed upon with the client at the beginning. As each method requires a different type of graphic expertise, it is best to determine which method is desired, and include the cost of end product in the budget. Three-ring binders, PowerPoint presentations, books (saddle stitch, spiral, coil, paperback, hardbound), videos, and slideshows are the standard methods. Make sure the event budget includes post-event consulting and preparation time.

Portions of the following case studies were used in award-winning contest entries, and reflect a collaborative effort between the client's representatives and The Lundquist Company. Often events are entered in event industry competitions as well as competitions of the client's respective industries. Competition entries are often a stated objective as the awards they garner bring attention to the client and are used by the marketing and communications departments.

RESULTS-DRIVEN EVENT CASE STUDY

BACKGROUND:

Established in 1874, the Matthew Kilgore Cemetery is one of the earliest pioneer cemeteries in the region. The cemetery land had been sold in the 1950s and years of neglect and ghoulish vandalism had made it a forgotten piece of Sacramento's California Gold Rush history. Descendents of those interred and local Scout troops had worked off and on to maintain the cemetery, but with little lasting impact. When the city of Rancho Cordova incorporated in 2003, the cemetery was within the new city boundaries. In 2005, the cemetery was donated to the city and a $1 million restoration project began. The completion of the project, which included installation of an ash wall for new internments, was cause for celebration. The city would stage an appropriate event, mindful of the respect a cemetery requires, yet suitably celebratory.

GOAL:
Announce the completion of a cemetery renovation.

STRATEGY:
An event was used as a public relations tool to draw attention to the newly renovated cemetery. The slightly quirky yet very colorful theme was a convergence of the pioneer roots of the cemetery and the Sacramento region's notable Dixieland Jubilee. We would stage a "lively" mock New Orleans jazz funeral with an undertaker, brass band, procession, speeches, music, food, and displays.

OBJECTIVES/RESULTS:
1. Gain media attention demonstrating that Rancho Cordova cares about its historic roots.
   ➡ Print, broadcast, and electronic media coverage (measurement using clippings and list of media hits).
2. Locate some of the 60 missing headstones from the 150 graves.
   ➡ Return of ten headstones, with three more identified for collection.
3. Locate as many of the cemetery descendants as possible to invite to the event and establish communication with family members on the future management of the cemetery.
   ➡ 150 of the attendees were direct descendants of the cemetery founders.
4. Promote the opportunity to be interred in the new ash wall.

- ➧ 17 interest cards regarding interment in the ash wall were picked up and two submitted to the city with a request for more information.

5. Cause descendants to be proud of the renovation and pleased with the city's stewardship.
   - ➧ More than 150 memory/thank you cards filled out at the event expressing joy at the cemetery's restoration and pleasure with the event (samples available for viewing).
6. Stage an event, mindful of the respect a cemetery requires, yet suitably celebratory.
   - ➧ Attended by 377 people, five times larger than originally planned.

CREATIVITY:

Using the jazz funeral as a vehicle offered a theatrical visual with built-in opportunities. City leaders were identifiable carrying parasols; three clergy (Catholic, Lutheran, and Christian) represented the spiritual side of the occasion; attendees participated in the parade; keepsake "second line" hankies and hand fans served dual purpose; bunches of flowers decorated the pine casket; and after the ceremony, flowers were retrieved by the attendees and placed on the graves of their loved ones.

BUDGET/PRODUCTION COSTS:

The original budget was to stage a monthly meeting at the cemetery. It included hiring an event producer, feeding 75 people at an off-site venue, providing sound, staging, and furnishings. When redesigned as a major public relations effort, the budget was increased. The themed event provided a vehicle for good will and a colorful participatory visual. In addition to attracting and accommodating a crowd five-fold the original estimate, positive media coverage, recovering tombstones, recognizing those interred, updating the descendants contact list, and publicizing the new ash wall, the public relations value is immeasurable.

AWARDS:
International GALA Awards, *Special Events Magazine*
Marketing
CAPIO Awards, California Public Information Officers
Association
Best Special Event
CELEBRATION Awards, CA Festivals and Events
Association
Best New Idea
CAPPIE Awards, Sacramento Public Relations
Association
Silver Cappie Best Special Event

RESULTS-DRIVEN EVENT CASE STUDY

BACKGROUND:
After a series of meetings with Rancho Cordova community representatives, a recommendation for celebrations of the fifth anniversary of cityhood was put forth. The committee

favored a large, community-wide, centralized event along with a series of outreach-oriented events prior to the main celebration. The plan included all segments of the residential and business population, and offered a variety of methods to reach the audiences. The primary focus was a festive celebration at City Hall on Tuesday, July 1, the actual anniversary date of incorporation.

GOAL:
Celebrate the fifth anniversary of the city of Rancho Cordova at City Hall.

STRATEGY:
Stage a series of neighborhood events building momentum to a big event held in the City Hall parking lot.

OBJECTIVES/RESULTS:
1) Attract families to a City Hall parking lot event on a weeknight in 100-degree weather.
   ➥ The free event was held at dinner time; shuttle buses brought people to the site from their neighborhoods.
2) Have food available the entire time of the event.
   ➥ After checking overhanging tree limbs and fire safety for outdoor grilling, calculations determined how many commercial barbecues would fit in the space, how many hamburger patties would fit on each grill, and how long it would take to cook the patties — we could serve 3,000 burgers during the event hours. Working from the number of 1,650 (guest count at the five neighborhood events), we confirmed 2,000 burgers. The caterer had an additional 1,000 patties in their cooler truck. In total, 2,360 burgers and veggie burgers were served

3. Make a parking lot look interesting without spending a great deal of money.

➤ The parking lot became visually interesting by adapting the elements of a beer garden (umbrella tables and Tivoli lights), big band shell (yellow Velon hung from a tent frame above the rented dance floor), food concessions (50 feet of hamburger service with "In" and "Out" signage), and linens in the bright colors of the "5th" logo.

4. Positive publicity for the city.

➤ Attendance of local, regional, statewide, national, and international dignitaries. Message points delivered verbally through the speakers, visually through photo displays and presentations, through the written word in the program, and printed take-home collateral. The "5th Anniversary" logo was branded throughout the city on signage, banners, advertising, staff t-shirts, and on the website. Guests received branded reusable bags filled with branded gift items. Media coverage, including a newspaper front-page color photo, acknowledged the event as being newsworthy.

CREATIVITY:

"Grass roots" neighborhood events: involve neighborhood committees and use of volunteers to cook hot dogs, talent from the high school, and the district's city councilperson. Hold events at dinner time; provide activities for young children and teenagers; provide seating for older folks. The big event, with dancing, burgers, dignitaries, activities, and entertainment, was well promoted at the individual neighborhood events. Attendance at each neighborhood event was between 200 and 500.

THE NUMBER FIVE:

The use of the number 5, a.k.a. "FIVE", was prevalent throughout all of the events. Five children, who just so happened to be five years old, were selected to pass the official cardboard torch from neighborhood to neighborhood, and all five children participated in passing the faux torch to the five-year-old child at the City Hall event. The torch idea sprouted from the upcoming summer Olympics and was a low-cost, fun vehicle to attract friends and family members to both the neighborhood and the City Hall celebrations.

INVITATION:

Four thousand invitations sent to residents incorporated the word "party" in four languages.

TELEVISION:

To reinforce the hometown spirit, a series of community-based television commercials featuring locals singing and saying "Happy Birthday."

BUDGET/PRODUCTION COSTS/VALUE:

To spend city funds for a "party" could raise questions — to spend the same amount on a six-week public relations campaign that kicked off a year-long branding effort and directly involved community participation was a solid investment. Community involvement can be seen directly in the budget line items of food and entertainment, which cost about 50% of the going rate. Production of the main event came in 20% under budget, while the attendance of more than 2,000 guests exceeded the original guest estimate of 500 - 750 by 266%.

AWARDS:
> International GALA Awards, *Special Events Magazine*
>> Nomination Best Corporate Event
>
> CAPIO Awards, CA Public Information Officers Association
>> Award of Excellence
>
> SUMMIT Awards
>> Creativity Award
>
> CAPPIE Awards, Sacramento Public Relations Association
>> Gold Cappie Best Corporate Event
>> Gold Cappie Community Relations

RESULTS-DRIVEN EVENT CASE STUDY

BACKGROUND:

In what we now refer to as Old Sacramento stands Engine Company No. 3, a brick firehouse built in 1853, which was home to a volunteer fire crew and California's first fire department. In 1960, the California historic landmark was renovated California Gold Rush style into a bar and restaurant.

From movie stars and politicians to world travelers and locals, the many functional rooms of the facility offer the perfect choice for special occasions. Ronald Reagan, held both
of his California governor inaugural dinners there, and more
recently, the Amgen Tour of California held a press conference announcing Sacramento's inclusion in the bicycle tour.
The charm and history of the restaurant have attracted distin-
guished guests for 50 years.

GOAL:
Design a festive evening celebrating 50 years of gourmet dining in Old Sacramento, which pays homage to The Firehouse
Restaurant's glamorous past and sets the stage for an exciting
future.

STRATEGY:
Invite 400 special guests to a five-hour party held in an internationally recognized Old Sacramento landmark, The Firehouse Restaurant.

OBJECTIVES/RESULTS:
1. Showcase the food, beverages, and impeccable service
   of the award-winning five-star restaurant.
   ➡ Serve different food and beverages in each room.
     Main Dining Room: Waiters in fedoras and
       white gloves passing silver trays of delicacies
       and champagne in flutes, an oyster bar featur-
       ing an ice carving with the 50th anniversary
       logo.
     Golden Eagle Room: Chateaubriand carving
       station, Lobster Thermidor, Quiche Lorraine,
       hors d'oeuvres, two wine bars.

Golden Eagle Salon: Passed hors d'oeuvres and the signature drink, the Firehouse Gold Martini, complete with a gold sugar rim.

Wine Cellar I: Formal "big business" meeting table display with a stack of real money, gold fountain pens, and a real guard dressed in old-school guard uniform.

Wine Cellar II: Foie Gras, Caviar, Beef Tartar, and a wine bar

Wine Cellar (bottle room): Variety of cheeses and a wine bar

Courtyard Grill: Fruit and cheese mountain and a full service bar

Courtyard: a flambé station serving Bananas Foster, a gelato cart, signature martini bar, two wine bars, a cappuccino bar

➡ Awards and plaques discreetly displayed.

2. Pay tribute to the history of both Old Sacramento and the converted firehouse built in 1853.

➡ Framed historic photos of the building.

➡ The venue is a favored spot of politicians and movie stars when in Sacramento. Many celebrity photos and special occasion photos are hung in appropriate rooms throughout the venue.

➡ Table #11 reset as it was for both of the inaugural dinners of Governor Ronald Reagan. Behind the table hung autographed photos of each dinner, and of then Governor Reagan and the First Lady in the restaurant.

3. Recognize 50 years in business while melding the past, present, and future.

➨ The building contains a labyrinth of rooms with seating for an intimate dinner for two up to a banquet for 300. Each room featured a different gold theme décor — signature gold martinis, gold nuggets under glass, gold fountain pens in wait of the signing of a big deal, gilded frames housing directional and informational signage, and hundreds of gold Mardi Gras beads.

➨ Room themes ranged from traditional to a lively modern party in the outdoor Courtyard toward the end of the evening.

➨ The attire of the food servers remained the same, as they would be moving from room to room throughout the night. The bartenders wore vests, ties, hats and tails appropriate to the theme of their room. The bartenders in the "high-roller" Golden Eagle Salon wore gold brocade vests, while the "modern" Courtyard bartenders were dressed in lime, fuchsia, and tangerine ties and vests with a geometric pattern.

4. Introduce the first private label wine.

➨ Formal presentations on the stage in the New-Orleans-style Courtyard were highlighted with the reveal of a 10-foot banner bearing the label of the restaurant's new wine release: Firehouse No. 3 Cabernet Sauvignon 2007.

5. Thank guests and reinforce the brand.

➨ Guests were greeted by valet parkers in black newsboy caps and six females in white tails flanking a red carpet.

➤ As they departed, guests received the crowning touch to the evening — two commemorative Riedel stemmed wine glasses etched with the 50th Anniversary logo and a picture of the Firehouse Restaurant.

JUST PLAIN FUN:

Over the years, the Firehouse has hosted a veritable who's who, including Ronald Reagan, who held his Inaugural Dinner when elected governor of the state of California, and Hollywood icons like Deano, Sammy, and Frank, who hung with the locals when in town. Imagine our guests' surprise when greeted by look-alike Sarah Palin with her secret service bodyguard in the Main Dining Room, and the Rat Pack crooning to the crowd in the Gold Eagle Room. Each room had a different theme and food, creating a surprise around every corner for the guests. The finale of the evening was held in the outdoor courtyard, where a tribute band played, and short speeches were given from the stage.

The theme "Hats Off to You" was evident in the sea of fedoras, cowboy hats, top hats, pillbox hats, headpieces, and even a pirate hat as guests embraced the spirit of the evening while swinging and swaying to the Sinatra tribute band. Cases of gold beads and colorful feather boas handed out by six-foot-tall twins in long gowns added a splash of fantasy to the already mesmerized crowd in the Courtyard.

Thematic guest experience:
- Gold elements in every room tied the theme together
- Wait staff in black suits, fedoras, and white gloves
- Exquisite floral arrangements throughout the restaurant
- Nine bars

- A Kabuki drop reveal of the new wine label
- A signature martini with a gold sugar rim
- A five-piece tribute band
- Four celebrity look-alikes
- Formally dressed guests in hats, including the mayor of Sacramento, the previous restaurant owner, several local television personalities, and the owner in a Stetson, all gave rise to a lively evening.
- Restaurant owner and guests alike marveled at the attention to detail, celebration grandeur, and the attention to tiny details.

AWARDS TO DATE:

CAPPIE Award, Sacramento Public Relations Association Gold Cappie Best Special Event

ESPRIT Award, International Special Events Association Nominee Best Corporate Event

RESULTS-DRIVEN EVENT CASE STUDY

BACKGROUND:

In 2003, The Lundquist Company was contracted to create a one-time event celebrating the fifth anniversary of First 5 Sacramento. The First 5 Sacramento Commission works to improve the lives of the county's youngest children and their families through an effective, coordinated, and inclusive implementation of the California Children and Families Act, also known as Proposition 10, which was enacted in 1998. The ultimate goal is to enhance the health and early growth experiences of children, enabling them to be more successful in school and to give them a better opportunity to succeed in life.

Since the commission grants money to local organizations and neighborhood groups, we suggested a resource expo be included in the event to showcase the groups and their projects.

The event was so successful that it became the annual signature event of First 5 Sacramento and has expanded every year.

GOAL:
To put a face on First 5 Sacramento in Sacramento County.

STRATEGY:
Stage a free, annual, family event that features First 5 Sacramento grantees and directly connects the grantees to their audience in the community.

The Saturday event was held in Fairytale Town, a conveniently located, gated, private children's amusement venue on the grounds of William Land Park in Sacramento. Free admission to Fairytale Town, 600 free bus passes, and free food were incentives to attract attendees.

An educational "resource expo" was installed in the park. It included booths from the First 5 Sacramento grantee organizations, community-based organizations (such as the library), and fire and police protective services.

The "Healthy Neighborhood" area showcased elements of a healthy lifestyle. Organizations reported excellent interaction with attendees and effective distribution of educational information (topics such as water safety and immunization). A fine-tuned marketing plan was designed to appear like a grass roots effort. Flyers were translated into Spanish, Russian, and Hmong and distributed to sites where parents take children, such as preschools and health agencies.

OBJECTIVES/RESULTS:

1. Educate parents and children using Educational Re source Expo
   ➡ 68 representatives of First 5 Sacramento grantee funding and community-based organizations with interactive booths, displays, activities; 6 hours of multicultural talent (11 acts); 938 children fingerprinted; 1,250 bags of books; and 35 library cards distributed
2. Attendance 6,000 (families with children under the age of five)
   ➡ 7,068 attendees; 51% children, 49% adults; 18% more attendees than measurable objective
3. Family fun in a park setting from 10 a.m. to 4 p.m.
   ➡ Free food, activities, entertainment, and resources for the entire family; 40,634 giveaway items; 5 entertainment activities; and 24 raffle prizes
4. Reinforce healthy habits
   ➡ Food menu approved by county dieticians; "Healthy Neighborhood" showcased gardening and vegetables; dentists in "Tooth Fairy Lane" conducted 1,053 first-time dental checks; 50 hearing tests in the mobile hearing van.
5. Sponsorship and partnerships
   ➡ Sponsorships (cash) and partnerships (in-kind value) enhance the event by subsidizing new ac-

tivities. This year, the signage costs, some tenting, and a new venue — the Baby Stop — were made possible through sponsorships and partnerships.

CREATIVITY/THE CHALLENGE:

The celebration is perceived as one festival but is actually two events taking place simultaneously, side-by-side, in two venues. We have two sets of contracts, insurance, permits, security, medical, talent, and event staff. Plus, it takes place outside at the beginning of the rainy season.

➡ Placing the expo tents in a circle around a giant tree (wrapped with a 30-foot coloring mural) allowed parents to visit the booths while keeping their eyes on the children coloring.

➡ Containing the free food inside the gates of Fairytale Town created built-in security against party crashers.

➡ Retailers exhibiting in the expo provided prizes for the main stage raffle.

➡ Police cars and a fire truck were positioned by the entrances to the expo. Uniformed representatives provided the illusion of security (at no cost to the event). Hired security was also on-site at all times.

➡ The signature element is the Mascot Conga Line. Midday, the Cat in the Hat (2010 Mascot Guest of Honor) led a block-long conga line of 26 costumed characters plus attendees from the fun inside of Fairytale Town to "Healthy Neighborhood," where they greeted children and posed for photos.

➡ NEW IN 2010:
   1) The Baby Stop, a safe haven for parents to change and nurse their babies.
   2) Immunization Clinic: 110 vaccinations and immunizations provided and registered.

BUDGET:
Total expense came in under budget (by $114) while serving 18% (1,068 people) more attendees.

AWARDS since 2003:
International GALA Awards, *Special Events Magazine*
    Best Festival: 2008, 2010
    Award Nominee: 2003, 2004, 2005, 2006, 2007, 2009

CELEBRATION Awards, CA Festivals and Events Association
    Best New Idea: 2003, 2005, 2006, 2008
    Best Marketing Campaign: 2005, 2006

ESPIRIT Awards, International Special Events Society
    Corporate Event: 2003
WESTIE Awards, West Coast International Special Events Society
    Best Corporate Event: 2004

CAPPIE Awards, Sacramento Public Relations Association
    Gold Cappie Best Special Event:
        2003, 2004, 2006, 2008
    Gold Cappie Best Bang for Buck (Baby Stop): 2010
    Silver Cappie Best Special Event: 2005, 2007, 2009
    Silver Cappie Best Festival: 2009
    Silver Cappie Public Relations Tool: 2009
    Bronze Cappie Best Festival: 2010

THERE IS NO DRESS REHEARSAL — CAN YOU HANDLE THE PRESSURE?

I read that some people are born with a gene causing them to be more daring than others. They love taking risks. They love hang gliding and bungee jumping. I believe people who choose the field of events as a profession have a gene that makes them shine when facing the worst of obstacles and thrive when others back away in fear. They are calm and in control when others are scattered in thought and incapable of making decisions. It's as if they were born for the challenge of the unexpected.

Watching an event professional at this work is a real time education. They all have different styles, some are outgoing and some shy, but deep down they are so focused on the task at hand you can almost see the wheels turning in their head. It's a pleasure, an honor, and simply invigorating to watch them function in what often seems like chaos. No matter what their area of expertise, they're in it for the long haul. They have the ability to see through the distractions to the end product, and don't get bogged down in the weeds. If they fall off the horse, they get back on and ride even faster.

Of course there are prima donnas and blowhards; every industry has them. There are industry icons, trailblazers, and the meek geniuses who retreat at the thought of being in the limelight. And, there are those of us who simply love what we do, and want to share our enthusiasm with those who want to learn about the industry. So, where do you fit in the scheme of things?

DO YOU HAVE THE STAMINA?

You might think that events are fun and exciting. They are, especially from the guest perspective. But the business of events is serious business.

Being an event professional takes continual training to stay current with the latest advancements in the industry. Keeping up with trends is a must as the colors and products of the fashion and design worlds quickly make their way to the event scene.

Are you a problem-solver? Can you focus on a single problem with mass excitement and energy whirling around you?

Are you a visionary who can turn an idea into a three-dimensional experience? Can you incorporate all five senses into your event? Do you have a sixth sense?

Are you a numbers person who instinctively knows how to adjust budgets to stay on track? After the planning is in motion, can you delete elements in the budget and still produce a great event?

WHERE ARE THE JOBS?

Being in the event business means wearing many hats and changing them often; it also means constantly testing and growing your capabilities.

There are so many job titles related to events that you don't have to be the planner, designer, director, or producer to get satisfaction from creating a spectacle. Florists, caterers, decorators, rental firms, and photographers all add their specialty to make the event shine. Security and fencing companies keep us safe, talent wows us, and transportation gets us from place to place. Tent companies and venues give us a place to hold our event, and the client gives us the reason.

Over the years, events have become an accepted part of the marketing mix and as such, new jobs have opened up for people with the interest and expertise to produce the events. Many colleges and universities have certificate programs.

Most hospitality and recreation and leisure studies programs offer classes on event planning and event marketing.

The opportunity to produce events has expanded to both likely and unlikely places of business, from formal annual awards ceremonies to casual outdoor product samplings. Many of today's households have both spouses working and no time to plan special occasion gatherings. There are clubs, churches, cause-related organizations, and professional associations holding events. The opportunity to become involved in events is all around you.

TIPS ON HOW TO ENSURE SUCCESS

As with a good book, a plane ride, and a meal, there is a beginning and middle and an end. The actual event is only the middle. It takes focused effort in the beginning and follow-through in the end to consistently produce results.

1) Build the event plan to understand the results the event is expected to accomplish.
2) Design the event to fulfill the directive of the plan.
3) Constantly reference your plan to make sure you're on track with your individual objectives and overall goal.
4) Manage the paper trail to keep your source documents in check.
5) Manage the people to keep the human element in balance.
6) Report the results honestly.
7) Present the results with clarity, in a manner in which your client will understand.

THE NEXT GREAT IDEA IS IN YOUR BATHTUB

Stuck thinking about a theme for this year's company picnic or the launch party for the new product? My suggestion is to forget about it. Stop fretting over an idea and go shopping or to a movie or a museum, or prune the rose bushes or cook spaghetti sauce or soak in a tub.

By the time you get stuck thinking, your head is full of so many discarded ideas that you need to shake out the cobwebs and allow more ideas to flow in. Like the ocean, the waves come in and the waves go out, but the mighty ninth wave is the one the surfers wait for. Embrace the ninth wave as a lesson in not falling in love with your first great idea.

Remember the last time you had the greatest idea and then the next day you had a better idea? Trust in yourself that your creative mind will deliver your next great idea. Purposely diverting your attention from the topic at hand and being stimulated by unrelated ideas allows the next great idea to easily bob to the surface.

I'm often asked, "What do you like about events?"

My answer is consistent, "I'm fascinated by the fleeting quality of events — spending hours, weeks, months, and sometimes years designing a guest experience that has a limited lifespan. It's like installation art. It's here and then it's gone. "

Simply said, I enjoy creating memories for the guests while boosting the bottom line for the client. That's exciting and that's what makes me happy, and it can work for you too. With a little practice you will please your client and receive recognition for your efforts.

Events can be complicated, but you can overcome all obstacles if you stay focused on the desired results. Being successful takes persistence, continually furthering your education, feeding your creativity, and having a targeted desire to make things happen.

Now you have the tools — it's time to put them to work.

ACKNOWLEDGMENTS

A really big round of applause to my friends and colleagues with whom I've worked on events over the years, and whose insight continues to nurture my passion for events: Gail Stewart, Paul Harris, Laurie Heller, Nancy Pearl, Erin Treadwell, Bridget Henderson, Kathy Newby, Susan Kidwell, Debra Payne, Erin Blount, Molly Watkins, Earl Godfrey, Desireé Pickert, Christy Wheeler, and to, all my colleagues at CalFest and ISES.

Congratulations for their fortitude go to friends who over the years have allowed me to drag them to any and every event under the sun, from citrus fairs and religious parades to coronations, and even a slug festival: Cathy MacMillan, Sue Torngren, Patt Sheldon, Marvin Salles, Flo Cavanaugh, Sabina Lewis, Barbra Riley, Lynn Guenard, Donna Shellooe, Karl Gerdes, Sheila and Jean-Claude Langer.

For letting me add my twist to their birthdays, weddings, graduations and other special occasions, a heartfelt thanks to Tom LaMair (1936-2004) and his family Temeca LaMair, Maxine Becker, Zaunia Sherman, Kelly, Eric, Rachel, Austin, and Erica Heikila, Terry LaMair, Kevin and Samantha LaMair, TJ and Stephanie LaMair, and their son, little "Tommy." Thomas John LaMair III — get ready for a lifetime of celebrations!

Special thanks to my writer friends for their encouragement: Jennifer Basye Sander, JT Long, and Janet Fullwood.

A huge thank you to clients who have entrusted their milestone occasions to me, and to all of you reading who love events.

COVER PHOTOGRAPH,
RESULTS-DRIVEN EVENT PLANNING

When considering images for the cover of *Results-Driven Event Planning*, there was no one image that captured the essence of a superior event. Extravagant table settings, huge tented installations, memorable themes, music and entertainment that had the party hopping, theatrical lighting, special effects, over-the-top florals, creative gourmet fare, and images of tears and smiles are all threads of the fabric from which a great event is woven, but no single image screamed "This is what successful events are all about."

Then, I asked myself, "What is the single image that says you are the best?" The answer was straight forward and easy. It's the image I am fortunate to see every day in my office. In fact, I have three. It's the icon that reminds me I am very good at what I do.

The greatest achievement in one's chosen profession is being selected by your peers as being the best. There is no higher recognition, and it is represented by the trophy that names you the award-winner. The trophy on the cover is called a Gala Award and is presented by *Special Events Magazine* annually in a number of categories for excellence in the special event industry. The meaningful Gala Award, a contemporary styled silver-plated pewter icon standing 13" tall on a polished marble base, is a created by MK Shannon. My thanks to Lisa Hurley, Editor, Special

Event Magazine, and M.K. Shannon, designer/owner, MK Shannon Awards, for allowing us to honor the event industry with use of this image.

Special Events Magazine, a Penton Media, Inc. publication www.specialevents.com 1-800-543-4116

The Gala Awards have been given by *Special Events Magazine*, the premier industry publication, since 1986, when the awards honored the "top 10 events of 1985." They recognize the finest work in special events worldwide. After three rounds of judging, winners are selected by members of the *Special Events Magazine* Advisory Board.

MK Shannon Awards www. mkshannonawards.com 1-800-542-8473 (US) or 530-271-1234 (Int'l)

For more than 25 years, MK Shannon Awards has designed unique custom awards for corporations, non-profits, associations and foundations. We are proud to help our clients recognize people and projects for their important contributions to their industries, and the achievements that inspire greatness in others.

ABOUT THE AUTHOR

Since 1980, Ingrid E. Lundquist, CSEP has been producing award-winning events, earning a reputation as a leader in creative solutions, innovative design, and accountable event management. Her firm specializes in the design and production of high-profile events for corporations and nonprofit cultural organizations. They are often called upon to produce one-time events such as groundbreakings, grand openings, and milestone celebrations.

The Lundquist Company is based in California's state capital, where Ingrid is past president of the local chapter of the American Marketing Association and Sacramento Public Relations Association. Ingrid is a current board member of CalFest (California Festivals & Events Association), and teaches *Results-Driven Events* for the University of California, Davis Extension, Marketing Certificate program. She is a member of the Northern California chapter of the International Special Events Society (ISES) and was the 109th person to receive the ISES designation of Certified Special Event Profession (CSEP).

Ingrid has a bachelor's degree and a master's degree in art and a bachelor's degree in english from California State University, Sacramento. She is author of three books and writes for industry related publications. Ingrid lives in Granite Bay, California where she dusts her ever-growing Statue of Liberty collection and tends a small vineyard.

email: i.lundquist@events-TLC.com   www.events-TLC.com

CPSIA information can be obtained at www.ICGtesting.com
Printed in the USA
BVOW031629301212

309190BV00005B/40/P